When Kids Were Allowed To Be Kids

Volume 1

When Kids Were Allowed To Be Kids

Volume 1

Stories by
Gary Schoolcraft

Railroad Street Press
394 Railroad Street, Suite 2
St. Johnsbury, VT 05819

All rights reserved by the author. No parts of this book may be copied or reproduced without the express written consent of the author.

Published in the United States by Railroad Street Press, St. Johnsbury, Vermont.

ISBN 9781936711185

1. Memoir/Short Stories

First Edition 2012

Railroad Street Press
394 Railroad Street, Suite 2
St. Johnsbury, VT 05819
(802) 748-3551
www.railroadstreetpress.com

Just Saying....

The, "Queen's English" is not apparent in any of these stories; this is intentional. I hope that my use of language adds to the reader's understanding of these stories, and gives a sense of what was important — good times with family and good friends.

Dedication

I would like to take a moment to thank all of the people that touched my life and made this book possible. With a special thanks going to my two brothers Greg and Dean and our neighbor Dave. Without those three there would be many blank pages in this book.

Table of Contents

Preface

In the Beginning	1
The Covered Wagon	5
The Ball Game	10
Bruce at a Glance and Random Thoughts	14
Dave & Wobbles	17
Cowboys & Indians	21
Hanging Around the Girl's Camp	25
New Rule	29
Early January Thaw	32
Pinky & Porky	37
Going To Church	41
Mom	44
Today's Child	50
Bye Peanut	56
Stay Away From the Brook	62
Fridays With Mom	65
Trigger	68
Hard Cider	72
Spelling	76
On All Fours	79
The Old Car Trunk Lid	82

The Brooding House	86
Greg the Cobbler	91
Something Green	96
A Ditch For All Seasons	101
Summer, "63"	107
Camp	113
The Ski Tow	118
A New Word	122
School Bus Blues	128
Doodle Bugs I Have Known	132
The Old, "38" Dodge Pickup	137
Two for One	144

Preface

All of the following stories were written about actual events that happened in my life while growing up in the small Vermont town of Peacham. I realize time has a way of changing some of the minor details but the overall picture will remain unchanged. I have written all of these stories as I remember them happening or in some instances as they were told to me. There is no order in which these stories appear; I write them as they return to my memory. So with that being said, please keep in mind, one store may be about a time when I was very young and the next about my teenage years. Also, in some of the stories, the names have been changed to protect the guilty.

Please take a few minutes to make yourself comfortable and let the following pages take you back in time. Back to a time different than the one we have now, a time before electronic games took over kid's lives. A time when kids were not only allowed to make up games they wanted to play but also the rules. It was also a time when kids had to make the things they wanted to play with……I truly hope you enjoy reading about life during the late fifties and all through the sixties as much as I enjoyed living them.

In the Beginning

Hello World.

Life, for me, began on a fall day in the first half of the 1950's. I was the oldest of three boys and grew up on my family's poultry farm in the small town of Peacham, Vermont. As far as I know Peacham was as good of a town as any to grow up in.

Many of the kids I grew up with lived on farms, mostly dairy farms, but the one thing we all shared in common was the lack of money. None of us had any. But that didn't seem to bother any of us or slow us down at all. Sure we were poor by today's standards but none of us

knew that................As I sit here searching for the next word to write I began to realize how much our world has changed in the few years I have been alive. I grew up in a time much different than the one we have now. The trouble is the change happened so slow that you didn't realize it was happening until it had already happened. And if you did notice the change there was always someone there to point out that it was only progress.

When I first started school, Peacham had three one room school houses with two grades in each school and Peacham Academy. Even though the seventh and eighth graders were not part of the academy until their freshman year they were housed in the same big old building.

The school house that held the third and fourth graders didn't have running water so one of the jobs our teacher had was to bring in a fresh jug of water every day. She would then pour that jug into the water cooler. All of us kids had our own paper cup with our initials on the bottom of them so we knew which cup to grab. After recess there was always a big line at the water cooler as we waited our turn. You never did dare to put your guard down while waiting in line because there was always one kid that would take his cup of water and pour it in someone's back pocket.

The lack of water also meant we had an outhouse instead of flush toilets. Us kids didn't think much about this until December and January rolled around and the temperatures dropped to below zero. This shortened the bathroom use at least by half.

Our town also had a ski tow which was run by an old ford flat head v-eight engine. Old telephone poles had been set in a straight line on the steep hill with car rims bolted to the top of them. At the foot of the hill was a shack just big enough to hold the car frame with the engine exposed for easy access to be worked on. An endless tow rope was laid on the car rims and went from the old ford engine to the top of the hill and back. Skiers had to grab onto this moving rope and squeeze until they started to move along with the rope, letting go when they reached the point where they wanted to get off. Also at the bottom was a ski shack which had a couple of picnic tables set up and a wood stove so the skiers had a place to grab a cup of hot chocolate or coffee, a hot dog or a bag of pop corn and warm up.

During this time us kids were also kept busy trying to come up with things to do to keep ourselves busy and out of our mother's way. For a while, my brother Greg, who was two years younger than I was, and I were busy building go carts. For some reason having a couple pieces of wood nailed together with wheels under it was high on our list of things to have. At first, our go carts were small and crude, but soon our building and design improved to where they were big and crude. After about the forth one we built we discovered one big flaw, these go carts had to be pushed. Our last go cart had three major improvements. It had a steering wheel and not just rope tied to each side of the front axle, a hand brake and an old chain saw engine. As it turned out the steering and brake needed a little more improving.

Since those early days the three one room school houses have been closed and there is now one large elementary school in the middle of the town. The academy graduated it last student in the spring of 71 and the old school building burned to the ground in 76. The ski tow no longer exists and the hill is now so over grown with trees that you would never know there was a time when the hill was alive with young people with long pieces of wood strapped to their feet, with bindings that did not release under any circumstance …… I can only assume all of these changes happened to make way for progress.

In the days, weeks and months ahead I would like to share with all of you stories about life during a time that, like the ski tow, no longer exists. A time that will soon be forgotten.

The Covered Wagon

My parents bought an old non working farm in the summer of 1958. This farm consisted of over thirty acres of land, a farm house with an attached garage and off that was an enclosed walk way to the barn. The barn which had partially burned at one time still had one section with a few stanchions for tying up cows There was another section used to house other farm animals such as pigs and sheep plus a large hay mow. At the end of the drive was a five bay tool shed which ran at a ninety degree angle with the drive way. Then off to one side of the tool shed was a small chicken coop which would probably house fifty or so chickens. This place ended up being home for my parents for more than forty years before they both passed away.

It didn't take my brother Greg and myself long to make friends with our closest neighbor, Dave. Dave was five years older than I was and it never ceased to amaze me how much knowledge he had acquired in the five years I wasn't around. In our eyes Dave knew everything. One of the first things Dave taught Greg and me to do was how to fill our cheeks full of air and let little bursts of squeaky air out so we sounded like Donald Duck. This used to irritate my Mom to no end, especially when the three of us came in from playing outside and she asked us if we would like a snack. The three of us would then stand there with our cheeks puffed out talking like Donald and trying to tell her what we wanted. As it turned out almost everything we did sooner or later rubbed Mom the wrong way. I remember one time Mom made the statement that it wouldn't hurt either one of us boys to get a little religion. Years later when she was reminded of her words she would shake her head and say, "I should have known better." But that is another story for another time.

Dave lived on the farm that was sandwiched between our house and the village. This farm had a very large field that ran from the edge of town to the valley below. Across the road from about the middle of this field was the farm house and a big three story brown barn along with several old tool and storage sheds. Dave's farm had a bunch of cows, two huge old work horses and a really big Billy Goat. I have long forgotten what Dave told me was the breed of his goat but it was huge and tipped the scales a bit more than two hundred fifty pounds.

After school, Greg, not yet old enough to go, would wait for my bus to arrive and then both Greg and I would wait for Dave to show up. We had a daily ritual of watching The Three Stooges and after a while each one of us assumed the identity of one of the Stooges. Dave was Moe, Greg was Larry and I was Curly. Moe was the one that was always smacking Larry and Curly in the back of the head and that was pretty much what life was like with Dave. We also watched a western; I think it was Wagon Train. When the show was over all we could talk about was riding in a covered wagon or galloping along on a horse, getting caught in a buffalo stampede or fighting outlaws. Then at the end of the day drinking hot coffee from a tin cup while sitting around an open fire.

Dave's Dad, Claude, had warned us about how hurt we could get if we ever tried to ride one of his cows and he said that was even before he got his hands on us, so we stayed away from the cows. The two old work horse's size alone prevented us from even trying to ride them. And then Dave's Billy Goat was just plain ugly. I mean whenever we saw Wobble's tongue come out and his ears lay back, all three of us would scatter in different directions and run for our lives. All the time, each of us praying that Wobbles had chosen one of the other two to run down and thrash.

Then one day Dave found an old wagon in one of the sheds. We dragged it

out and by using old burlap grain bags we were able to make the old wagon into our own personal covered wagon and it even looked a little bit like the ones on TV. One Saturday morning Dave showed up with the covered wagon with one of the old work horses hooked to the front of it. Greg and I took no time at all in climbing on board and as we were leaving the dooryard Mom came out with a lunch she had packed for us along with a large thermos of hot chocolate.

    We were going to do what we called the Ha Penny loop. Ha Penny connected Penny Street with the Mack's Mtn. Road and would loop us through the village and back home. Our plan was to wait until we hit the mile and a quarter long Ha. Penny Road before we dug into the hot chocolate and lunch our mom had made for us. Dave could let go of the reins and enjoy his lunch while the old work horse plodded along this seldom used road. No sooner had we started to eat our sandwiches when we heard the dreaded whooooooosssh. That miserable old horse waited until we were trying to eat our lunches before he released some gas he had been storing up for an occasion just like this. It seemed like every time we opened our mouths to take a bite the horse would let another blast go. I don't know if any of you have ever been around an old horse with digestive problems, but it makes eating your lunch all but impossible. It was awful and lasted just as long as our lunch did. I swear at one point that miserable old horse turned his head and gave us a big yellow tooth grin. Dave promised both Greg and me that he would get even with the horse and fix it so that he wouldn't be able to do that again.

The following Saturday, when Dave arrived, we noticed that he taken a long two inch wide leather strap and fastened it to one side of the harness that ran down the back of the horse. He then continued this strap down around the back of the old horse under his tail and hooked the other end of the strap to the harness that ran down the other side of the horse's back. This anti gas strap sure did look like it would work. Only later did we find out that we were wrong.

As soon as we hit the Ha Penny Road and reached for our lunch we discovered that all this strap did was give this horse something he could vibrate against his back side. By the time we returned from that trip the horse had convinced the three of us that riding in a covered wagon wasn't all that much fun after all, so we moved onto the next thing on our list. Goat riding.

The Ball Game

One beautiful summer day right after dinner both Greg and I ran outside to enjoy the few hours of daylight that was left. The moment we stepped out of the laundry room door into the garage our bikes seemed to be calling to us to ride them. Neither Greg nor I had a clue as to where we should go so we just jumped onto them and headed out of the dooryard. When we got to the end of the driveway our bikes automatically steered us down the hill, just like they had a secret navigation device hidden in them. Both Greg and I just worked our legs up and down on the pedals and the bikes took us to the intersection where Ha Penny and Penny streets intersected. At this intersection there were two houses, one being a farm house and the other not. Both houses were home to big families each having five to six kids. In the farm house, the youngest was a girl my age, and across the street was a family whose oldest was a year younger than I was.

When Greg and I arrived all the kids, from both houses, were outside just milling around, a few of them throwing stones and dried clumps of dirt that looked like a small bomb going off when they hit a tree or the road. I don't know how I can describe the feeling aside from saying you could feel the excitement building in the air as more kids showed up, some from as far away as three miles. Even the two farm dogs were running between the growing number of kids, not wanting to be left out of whatever was about to happen.

It wasn't long before there were kids of all ages running around ranging in age from a couple of five year olds to a few that were in their late teens, both boys and girls. Before long someone said we have enough here for a baseball game. Almost instantly a couple of baseballs appeared as did a few bats and countless gloves. A couple of the older teenagers became self chosen team leaders and they started to pick their teams, with each team leader taking a turn. Back then we were allowed to choose teams and the worst player was always chosen last. Everyone knew who the last person was going to be including that person. In this case it was Bruce. Bruce knew he would be chosen last even behind the two five year olds. Bruce was a year younger than I was and no one had ever seen Bruce hit a ball. Bruce claimed he hit a ball once but there was no witness so regrettably it had be ruled an unofficial hit. Bruce would spend hours throwing the ball up in the air and try to hit it as it came down. Several kids even stopped at Bruce's home while he was out behind the house honing his batting skills but not a soul ever saw him hit the ball. All they ever saw Bruce do was to strike himself out.

As the teams were being chosen you could see Bruce count the kids and do the math to see which team he would be on. Shortly one of the team leaders was seen smiling at the other one. He too had done the math. Before long both teams had been chosen and then the traditional bat toss to see which team would bat first. When that was over the batting line up was set, Bruce of course was once again last.

Finally after about three innings it was Bruce's turn to bat. Bruce grabbed a bat and took his place at home plate. Bruce took a few practice swings and then looked at the pitcher. In the mean time the outfielders had come in and were almost on top of the kids at first, second and third base, each anticipating an easy strike out. The pitcher pulled back and let the ball fly toward Bruce. At the last possible second someone yelled, "Swing Batter Swing." Bruce gave it all he had and there was this really loud KRRRRACK that echoed up and down the valley below. Bruce just stood there, with his mouth open and the bat still in his left hand with one end resting on the ground, as he watched the ball sail over the pitcher's head and the head of second baseman. The center fielder had turned around and was running as fast as he could to try to catch up with the ball. Finally someone, I think it was one of the five year olds, yelled, "Run Bruce Run." (Bruce would hear those exact same words again but not until he was in high school. One day a teacher thought Bruce had done something wrong and told him that he would have to stay after school. Bruce claimed he had been set up and would not stay after school. As soon as the final bell rang Bruce was out the door running for home. There was a bunch of us kids on the store porch when Bruce went flying by. Moments later the teacher, in her car, went by. All of us kids started to yell at the top of our lungs, "Run Bruce Run." The teacher caught up with Bruce on the flat just outside of the village limits. Bruce circled the teacher's car twice then headed cross country.) Bruce dropped the bat and took off for first base. When he reached first there was someone there to motion him onto second base. Bruce made about six steps toward second when this black blur came running from behind one of the trees. It was one of the farm dogs, which was about half the size of Bruce, and this dog nailed Bruce and knocked him to the ground. Bruce quickly was up on all fours but the dog had already mounted him, with romance on his mind. Instantly the other five year old yelled, "Crawl Bruce Crawl."…………..All of us kids were laughing so hard that both Bruce and the dog made it safely to second base. And Bruce's long standing record had been broken.

Bruce at a Glance and Random Thoughts

After writing the Ball Game story I thought Bruce deserved a little closer look, so here are a few of my memories of Bruce.

Unfortunately Bruce never did find a sport that he was really good at. I dare guess that if irritating teachers ever did become a sport he would have lettered in that one though. I remember one teacher that would give Bruce a quarter just so Bruce would go the store and get out of his hair, so to speak. I also remember in gym class one day we were playing basketball. A really big kid by the name of Burt was bringing the ball down the court and Bruce was trying steal the ball but instead tripped himself and fell to the floor. Burt ended up stepping on Bruce and he too fell but landed right on top of Bruce. Poor Bruce had the wind knocked out of himself and had to crawl off the court, all the time being yelled at to get out of the way. I'll bet it was fifteen minutes before Bruce was able to return to the game and again Bruce tried to steal the ball from Burt. I am not sure what happened this time but Burt ended up slamming

When Kids Were Allowed to be Kids

into the wall, or I should say he would have if Bruce wasn't between Burt and the wall. Again Bruce dropped to the floor gasping for air. He never did return to the game after that one.

Bruce, however, wasn't the only kid that ended up being abused while playing ball. One other time when we were playing basketball in the gym and a kid by the name of Bill went running to try to save the ball which was headed for the stairs. I heard the awful scream of fear and looked up just in time to see Bill's feet all tangled up, in a big yellow basketball net that was used to carry all the balls to the court, disappear down the stairs. Moments later all we heard was a bunch of moaning. Someone finally yelled to Bill to throw the ball back.......Then in little league one evening we were getting in a little practice before the opposing team showed up. For some reason Bobby B. decided to play catcher, usually Bobby was on second base. Bob had on the catcher's chest protector, face mask and catcher's mitt. I have forgotten who was at bat but they swung with all they had at the ball. They did get a piece of the ball but it was the very top corner and drove the ball almost straight down and when it bounced up it came up under the flap that hung between Bobby's legs, making a horrible noise when it hit Bobby. Bobby just stood up, with his eyes wide open and started this slow child like waddle to the bench. About half way there the glove fell off Bob's hand. Finally Bobby made the bench and all he did was sit down and hold his head in his hands. Never once did he ever let out a squeak or any noise at all……At one fourth of July baseball ball game I was catcher and Greg the pitcher. The batter hit a fly ball between Greg and me and we both took off after it. Thank god I never took my mask off because Greg and I collided. I had to sit out the next couple of innings and Greg had to go to the ER. He still wears the scars………

In the end Bruce did find his niche in life. After high school Bruce joined the Army. Unfortunately life was not kind to Bruce and he died a young man. He was buried in Arlington National Cemetery with full military honors.

Dave & Wobbles

This picture first appeared in a popular Vermont magazine sometime during the late fifties. Beside the picture were the words that went something like, "Freckled farmhand Dave is met at the bus stop by his pet goat Wobbles." Before I type another word I believe it is important for the reader to know that Wobbles was as common a sight in the small town of Peacham as was the store or the library. Wobbles was

always with Dave and the other kids in town and like all the other kids everyone knew Wobbles by name. It was also well known that Wobbles was not one of the better acting kids either

Dave got Wobbles when he was just a baby and raised him to the animal many residents of Peacham still remember. By the time Wobbles became full grown he tipped the scales at a little more than 260 pounds and had a mind all his own. Some might have gone as far as to call him stubborn but us kids only knew him as Wobbles.

Dave even had a small wagon made just for Wobbles and often would hook Wobbles up and ride the wagon to Peacham village. Once there Dave would just jump out and start to play ball or hide & seek or whatever other game happened to be going on at the time. One day, after Dave and Wobbles had been in the village for a while, one of the other kids said, "Where's Wobbles?" Dave and the other kids looked up and down the street and behind a few of the houses but Wobbles was nowhere to be found. Dave spoke up and said, "Well he probably got bored and went home." So with that in mind Dave started the walk home keeping an eye out for Wobbles. Right outside of the village limits there was a huge field which was part of Dave's farm. Cutting this field in half was a ditch that was about ten feet across and six to seven feet deep. Well in the bottom of the ditch is where Dave found Wobbles and the wagon. For some reason Wobbles thought that being in the bottom of the ditch was the place he wanted to be and that is where he was, stuck tight.

Once in a while, well to be honest with you often Wobbles would get out and walk to the village on his own, usually looking for some kids to play with. However on this particular beautiful romantic spring day Wobbles had something else on his mind. He happened to walk up behind a woman, we shall call Marion, for the purpose of this story. Marion was about in front of the library when she felt something nudge her from behind, evidently a form of foreplay to a goat. Rumor has it that the people in East Peacham, a village about a half a mile away, could hear Marion's screams as Wobbles continued with his fantasy. Much to Wobbles disappointment his next date was with a veterinarian.

The operation Wobbles had did calm him down a bit but he still had a mind of his own. Dave showed Greg and myself how to make a harness out of old bailing twine and how we Wobble's head and use it for reins. Wobbles didn't seem to mind much when Dave rode him but whenever Greg or I tried it was a different story. Wobbles always stood calmly while he watched us make the harness and would even stand still while we slipped it over his head. I think he did this to give us a false sense of confidence because the moment either Greg or I jumped on his back, all of that changed and in a hurry. Both Greg and I would spend days trying to ride Wobbles but neither one of us got very far. We did however get a bunch of bruises. Neither Greg or I could figure out how Mom knew we had spent the day trying to ride Wobbles. Greg or I never noticed it at the time, but goats don't smell that good.

After Dave finished high school he went to college and his dad, Claude, could not, due to his age, continue with the farm and was forced to sell off all the cows. He did however hang onto the two old big work horses and of course Wobbles. After college, the army thought they wanted Dave for a while so off to boot camp he went. While on leave from the service Dave would sit on the front porch and watch Wobbles sneak up on the work horses, take aim and charge one of the horses and butt him in the belly. Wobbles would then run for all he was worth and slide under the fence to get away from the horses.

    Wobbles was always Wobbles and never changed even to the day he died. Dave happened to be home on a ten day leave from the service. Two days before Dave was to leave for Vietnam he had to bury Wobbles. Many wondered if Wobbles couldn't stand the thought of Dave having to go to war................

Cowboys & Indians

As soon as dinner was finished during the warm evenings of summer, Greg and I would bolt from the dinner table, grab our hats and run outside. Even though the day was dying we knew we had several more hours to play outside and our choices of games were endless. Some nights we raced our bikes, played ball, marbles, hide & seek and many nights found us working on one of the countless go carts we built. This particular night found us playing cowboys & Indians. Our dooryard was the perfect place to play this game. We had a big old barn, a five bay tool shed and an old chicken coop in which we could hide. The chicken coop was really neat, it was of the old design of a one pitch roof. This allowed for plenty of room for large windows in the front so the sun could beat in and let the chickens dust themselves, something chickens all over the world love to do. Parked right behind the coop was an old dodge pickup that hadn't run for years, which was also fun to play in. Mom even encouraged us boys to play on the pickup and coop. Her exact words, if I'm not mistaken were,

"Don't let me catch you boys climbing on top of that old truck so you can get on the roof of the chicken coop or I'll tan your hides."

On this particular night Greg was going to be the cowboy and I was the Indian. I grabbed a six and a half foot long maple sapling which we used for a spear and Greg put on the six shooter. I ran around the end of the house and Greg, still with a slight limp, headed towards the old tool shed. A few days earlier, when Greg and I were working on one of our go carts, Greg was swinging a hammer driving in nails when he missed and bounced the head of the hammer off one of his legs about half way between his knee cap and ankle. This dropped him like he had been shot dead except he was flopping around on the garage floor and all kinds of odd noises were coming out of him. The next morning Greg had one of the biggest black and blue marks I had ever seen. It was a little bigger than a silver dollar and really black and according to Greg really sore.

As I rounded the corner of the house, I kept on running until I was on the back side of the barn. I then squeezed through a small opening on the back side of the barn and picked my way to the ground floor. I then found the perfect place to hide. This hiding place was dark and there were even a few cracks in the old barn boards so I could see the entire dooryard and one corner of the old tool shed. All I had to do was wait for Greg, the cowboy, to come looking for me and it would be an easy ambush from this hiding spot.

After sitting for at least fifteen to twenty minutes I began to think that maybe Greg had changed the rules and not told me. Usually the cowboy hunted the Indian but I thought that maybe Greg's leg still hurt too much to do all the running around that the hunter usually did. I gave it another five minutes before I convinced myself to go looking for Greg.

Using the shadows of the setting sun as cover, I finally made my way out of the barn. I then checked out the old tool shed, the chicken coop and made a double check of the barn, but Greg was nowhere to be found. In silence, I continued my search for another ten minutes and then even made a few subtle noises trying to flush him out but nothing worked. All the time I was getting really angry to think I couldn't find Greg. Finally I was standing by the corner of the tool shed when I yelled out, "Okay Greg you win." Still not a peep from Greg, so again I yelled out, "Didn't you hear me, you win."

I think Greg knew this was a well used trick just to get the other one to come out of hiding and then the battle would be on, so he didn't fall for it this time. Well by then I was mad and yelled at the top of my lungs, "I QUIT" and I threw my spear over the top of the chicken coop roof. About millisecond after the spear disappeared over the roof of the chicken roof I heard an awful scream followed by an odd thumping noise. Less than a second later I saw Greg bouncing along on one leg, holding the one bruised leg in one hand and the spear in the other. Greg stopped at the edge of the roof and took aim at me. Greg is a deadly shot so I didn't dare take my eyes off the spear and it was a good thing I didn't . I had to jump hard and roll to my left and then I was up running in a zig zag manner. I ran back to my hiding place and waited for Mom to call us in for the evening.

Later that evening, after Greg cooled off, he said he was laying on the roof holding his nose with one hand, with his other hand over his mouth trying not to laugh to give his hiding place away. That is when he saw a spear come flying over the roof and hit him right dead center in the black and blue on his bad leg.

Hanging Around the Girl's Camp

The summer of my nineteenth year found me back working on the family poultry farm; high school was behind me as was a short stint in college. My grandfather was retiring from the poultry farm, a farm he started back in the 1940's and I was going to try to fill his shoes. We no longer had birds on the farm, instead there was a big poultry farm in Bethel, Maine that we bought nest run eggs from. My job included making trips to Maine to pickup truck loads of eggs, bring them back to our processing plant in Peacham where they were washed, candled and packaged. I would then distribute them to our customers. I was on the road four days a week selling eggs and my favorite day on the road was Friday, or at least during the summer months it was.

On Fridays I delivered eggs to a bunch of summer camps around two lakes in the town of Fairlee, Vt. And one of these camps was a girl's camp, I think the name was Camp Lanakila. The older girls, all about my age, stayed in small cottages behind the main camp and had to walk right past the back of the kitchen to get to the dining hall. I had my egg route timed so I got to Lanakila right at lunch time. I had to drive behind the main camp to deliver the eggs through the back kitchen door and by being there right at noon time all the girls had to walk past my delivery van, something that worked in my favor.

On this particular Friday I happened to be a few minutes early so I decided to kill a little time. To do this I spent a couple of extra minutes talking with the head cook when I checked on their stock of eggs. When I thought the time was about right for the girls to start their walk I went out to the delivery van to get a case of eggs. This delivery van had both side and rear doors. To get the eggs that the cook wanted I had to go in through the rear doors of the van. I grabbed the door handle and gave it a twist upwards to open the door. I then jumped into the van and worked my way to the eggs I needed. I lifted the case of eggs and by sliding them across the top of other cases of eggs I was finally able to reach the back of the van. I had the eggs on top of another case of eggs half in and half out of the van. With my butt I bumped the door out of the way and I jumped out of the van grabbing the case of eggs in one smooth motion, something I had done countless times before. Then as soon as my feet hit the ground, I would walk the eggs into the camp's cooler. Trouble is my feet never hit the ground.

It was a few agonizing seconds, which felt much longer, before I was able to figure out what had gone wrong. The door handle, which was pointing straight up had slipped between my belt and pants. By holding the case of eggs off to one side I was able to look down and see that my feet were five or maybe six inches from touching the ground. My feet however were slowly inching their way closer to the ground but it was getting increasingly uncomfortable, besides that I had another problem, the girls were, any second now, going to start their walk to the dining area. I thought, for a quick second, that if I just hung there and didn't move they wouldn't see me but I had to rule that idea out. I tried to slide the case of eggs back into the van but each time I tried the door would swing. By then the back of my pants were between my shoulder blades and my breathing had become shallow. Quickly I checked on the girls again and so far my luck was holding out on that end. Out of desperation I started to swing the case of eggs from side to side and when I had a good momentum going I swung them into the back of the van. Luckily one corner of the case of eggs landed on top of another case and by grabbing the top of the van I was able to slide the eggs into the van. That allowed me to have both hands free to try to get off the door handle. Unfortunately I had hung on the handle so long that the back of my pants was high enough that I couldn't raise myself enough to get off the handle. In one last ditch effort I gave it all I had and slipped off the door handle and fell to the ground.

About that time the girls were starting their noon time walk. I quickly grabbed the eggs and did the toe to heal walk into the cooler. I didn't want the girls to see me with the back of my pants covering my shoulder blades. The moment I got in the cooler, I started to re adjust things to a more comfortable level. I know I was beet red in the face when I walked out of the cooler and I talked in a much higher tone but the cook didn't seem to notice.

New Rule

Growing up on a farm meant there was never any shortage of chores to do. One job that came around every year, during Christmas vacation, was to shovel all of the hen manure out of the hen houses that had been building up for six months and there was a lot of it. These hen houses were closed up tight during the winter months to try to keep all of the heat inside, so it was very stuffy inside these buildings to say the least. Whenever you walked inside one of the hen houses, after the shoveling had begun that is, the first thing you noticed was the horrible chicken manure smell and a very strong ammonia odor, a byproduct of the hen manure. This ammonia odor was so strong that your eyes would water so bad for a good five minutes that it was all but impossible to see. The next piece to this story is my brother Greg. Greg has the unique ability to absorb and mimic any smell he has been in, which made for many interesting situations. The only exception being anything that smelled nice.

One night during the first week of vacation my whole family was in the living room watching TV. As

I sat watching the tube my eyes began to water so bad that I had to wipe them. In a matter of seconds this horrible smell hit me, out of habit I looked at Greg and he sat in the chair grinning. Moments later the bad air reached Dad and instantly he began to yell at Greg. I mean he went up one side of him and down the other. Dad let Greg know that under no circumstance was he ever to let gas like that go again. Dad was mad and continued with, " If you even think you might have a bubble brewing you are to go to the bathroom and stay there until there is no question but it has gone." Much to my surprise Greg just took this tongue lashing. Usually Greg tried to defend himself but I guess this time even Greg knew there was no defending this one.

After a week or more of shoveling from morning to night Dad's back grew tired and began to ache real bad. One night Greg and I were again watching TV when Dad came walking, from the den through the living room, kinda hunched over a bit, holding one hand on the small of his back. Dad then headed towards the bathroom and started to draw a tub of real hot water. This bathroom was, as was most bathrooms in old farm houses, only big enough for a sink, stool and an old claw foot open bath tub. We then heard Dad go upstairs. A few minutes later Dad hobbled downstairs and was kinda humming a bit as he walked through the living room, carrying clean clothes. He then opened the bathroom door and disappeared into the steam that drifted out.

Greg and I continued to watch TV for a few more minutes when Greg stood up. Greg smiled at me, grabbed the top of his pants and gave them a little twist and headed to the bathroom. A hand full of seconds after Greg stepped into the bathroom I heard a bunch of yelling. It started off with a few swear words, then Greg's name was mentioned, then more swears mixed in with other words. Moments later Greg returned to his seat and said, " I go outside from now on."

Early January Thaw

One year during the first half of the 60's, winter came early and pounded us with a lot of cold weather and a lot of snow. The January thaw that year was also early. One day during Christmas vacation the temperatures started to rise and by late morning it felt like a beautiful warm spring day. But then the rains came and the snow started to settle to the point where you could once again see the top 5 to 6 inches of the fence posts in the fields. By late afternoon a cold snap moved in, the rains stopped and the temperatures dropped close to the single digits.

After dinner and baths, the night found all of us sitting in the living room watching TV. The TV sat on an outside wall facing the road between two windows. As we all watched TV a set of lights appeared in one of the windows, shone on one wall and slowly circled the room and went out the other window. About a second or two later, the light did the same thing. Dad got up and looked out one of the windows and said there was a car spinning around and around going down the hill. Instantly we all got dressed and went running outside. As soon as we stepped out of the garage we found everything covered with a thick coating of ice. The dooryard was a solid sheet of ice so Mom decided it would be better to walk across the lawn out to the road so she could see what happened to the car. As soon as she rounded the corner of the house her feet went out from under her, she landed on her back side and slid at an alarming rate of speed down to the road. Greg and I just looked at one another and smiled.

As it turned out, it was a state police cruiser that had been going down the hill doing 360's. The car was about half way down the hill with the back end buried in the snow in the big field across the road from our house, the very field Greg and I knew we would be sliding in come morning. Mom, Greg and I stood under the big trees in front of our house while Dad inched his way down to see if he could help the police out of their car. Off in a distance, towards the village, we could hear what sounded like a town truck coming our way, but it was moving very slowly. After a few minutes we could see some lights appear on the horizon and then we could see the outline of the town truck. Its dump body was up and the town men were spreading salt as the truck inched along. I still can remember the clatter of the tire chains as they slapped the road with each revolution of the tires. About the time the truck passed our driveway that sound was replaced with a scraping noise as the truck took off and started to spin out of control going slowly down the hill. All of the ice didn't seem to slow Dad or the two police men down at all as they took off running down the hill. When the town truck went by Mom, Greg and I could see the road foreman sitting in the driver's seat holding onto the steering wheel like it was going to save him or something. The truck did finally come to a stop but not until after it hit the cruiser.

    The next morning, after breakfast, Greg and I stood at the top of the big field holding a toboggan staring at the far lower corner wondering if we dared to try it. The sun was out and the crust shined so bright that it hurt our eyes. Finally, after a bunch of encouraging talk between ourselves, Greg stuck his feet under the front curve of the toboggan and I climbed on behind him. With a few pushes with our hands we were off. Almost instantly we were going so fast that the wind in our face made our eyes water. Evidently, about a third of the way down the hill, Greg got scared and he jumped off, claiming he fell off by mistake. When Greg jumped off the toboggan slid sideways which dumped me off. The toboggan then continued all the way down to the foot of the hill and disappeared into the woods.

    Greg and I had to walk all the way down to the far corner and then into the woods to get the toboggan. The crust was so thick that we could walk on top most of the way but once in a while we would find a soft spot and break through and our foot would sink into the deep snow.

On the long walk back to the top of the hill I made the suggestion that we should tie the rope we use to tow the toboggan to one of our legs, that way if we fell off the toboggan wouldn't go all the way to the bottom again. I assumed we would tie the rope to Greg's leg but as he pointed out, it was my turn to be up front and it would be better on my leg. It kinda made sense to me so that is what we did. Again we took off, only this time I was in front. We only got a little further down the hill before Greg accidentally fell off again and, like before, the toboggan slid sideways and dumped me off also. As luck would have it, I landed on one of the soft spots and broke through the crust. About two or maybe three hundredths of a second later, the rope tightened and the toboggan yarded me out of the hole and dragged me a good twenty feet down the hill before coming to a stop. Every inch of me hurt beyond belief and all I could hear was Greg laughing. That was the end of sliding for that day.

Monday morning, Mom loaded the car up with Greg and me and we took off for St. Jay Center. Mom's Dad, Grandpa Dick, owned a mink farm and Mom helped Grandpa get the pelts ready for market. While Greg and I were at Grandpa's, we spent our time playing with our cousins Richard and Janie and Richard's closest friend Billy. St. Jay Center, like Peacham, was covered with ice and once again we just had to go sliding. Luckily, right behind the mink farm, there were two very steep, but not very long, hills facing one another. On the back side of one of these hills was a very long and fairly steep hill that some farmer used to pasture his cows during the summer months. It was this field that we decided to slide on. Billy, full of excitement, was the first one to jump on his sled. He pointed the sled down the hill and sat upright on it and in a flash he was off. About half way down the hill Billy's sled hit a soft spot and broke through; the sled came to an abrupt stop, Billy did not and kept going down the hill only without the sled. Richard and I were standing side by side and we could see the top of a fence post sticking up and Bill was headed straight for it spread eagle. As Richard and I stood there watching we could see Billy with his arms behind him try to steer himself out of the way. At one point we could even see the rooster tail of snow spray up as Bill dug his fingers tips into the crust trying to slow down. Finally I looked at Richard and said, "That's gonna hurt." Moments later Billy slammed into the fence post spun around it and continued to the foot of the hill on his back.

Pinky & Porky

A few years after we moved to the old farm that Greg and I along with our youngest brother Dean grew up on, Dad bought a couple of pigs to raise. For a couple of days early one spring, Dad worked in the barn and built a special pen to hold the pigs and for several years after that we got two piglets each spring to raise. Each year Greg and I would name these pigs Pinky and Porky.

In the beginning of each year these pigs were fun to watch and to feed but within a couple of weeks they became just pigs and something Greg and I had to take care of, robbing us of fun things to do. After a couple of months these pigs had grown so much that both Greg and I thought they were big enough to ride. And the good news was these pigs were confined to a pen and there weren't any hard rocks to land on when they bucked us off. Something Dave's goat, Wobbles, took great pride and enjoyment in doing.

Neither Greg or I had enough nerve to get in the pig pen and try to ride one of these, by then, huge pigs. So with fear holding us back and stupidity egging us on we came up with what we considered the perfect plan. One of us, Greg, would stand in front of the pig pen and feed them vegetables from the garden. We found out early on that both Pinky and Porky loved vegetables, with the exception of radishes. Both pigs hated radishes with a passion and as soon as they bit into one of them they would spit it out with so much force that the radish would shatter when it hit a wall or one of us. Our plan was for Greg to keep the pigs busy eating veggies while I quietly climbed up on the pen and dropped silently, like a bobcat from a tree, onto one of the pigs. And this is exactly what this pig must have thought because he reared up on its hind legs spun around on his rear legs and took off like a shot for the other end of the pen. I took that moment, that the pig was on his hind legs, to wrap my arms around its neck and squeeze with all the strength that I had, which I am sure the pig took as a sign that the bobcat was about to rip the life out of him……. For those of you that don't know, all pigs are very clean animals, as far as it comes to going to the bathroom that is, and only relieve themselves in one corner of their pen, and that is as far as I got before the pig threw me.

    The landing knocked the wind out of me and I couldn't understand how Greg could find this funny, but he did. After Greg got done laughing he sneaked into the house, up to my room and brought me clean clothes, while I stayed hidden in the barn. I didn't think Mom, finding me covered with pig dung from head to foot, would help her mood out that much. I then changed into clean clothes and put the dirty ones in the hamper. Much to both Greg's and my surprise, Mom by dinner time, had figured out what we had done.

One summer, one of the pigs got this awful rash on its belly and we had to put this stuff that looked and smelled a lot like iodine on its stomach. I, being the oldest, was nominated to be the one that had to paint the pig's belly. Dad took an old coffee can put a couple of small holes in the top and used a piece of wire to make a handle. Then every night, as soon as Dad got home from work, he would climb into the pig pen and grab the pig with the rash by the front legs and pick it up, something the pig did not like at all. I would have the coffee can full of iodine and a paint brush and try to paint the pig's belly with the iodine. One evening the pig kicked the coffee can and the iodine went all over me. The iodine covered my face, neck and arms which in turn left me stained for days......Which reminds me, I think that was the summer that turned so hot that we almost had a drought. Every day the sun came out and baked everything outside. I remember Mom mentioning what a beautiful dark tan Greg was getting and actually envied him a bit. Early one evening mom opened the door and yelled out at Greg and me, interrupting a game of baseball, that dinner was ready. At the dinner table Mom looked across the table at Greg and noticed something that didn't look right on his neck. Mom got up from the table, grabbed a wet wash cloth and washed off most of Greg's tan.

Going To Church

The story I am about to share with you is one I don't remember, but I have heard my Mom live countless times.

Sometime during the winter months after I had turned six years old and Greg was four, Mom decided that it wouldn't hurt either Greg or me to get a little religion. The church in Peacham was a very old and large building, one with very high ceilings, built a

long time before insulation was popular or maybe even thought about. As it turned out that winter also happened to be one of the extremely cold winters that hit our region during the late 50's and early 60's.

The first Sunday that Greg and I went to church, Mom took us and it did not turn out too well and by the time we got home Mom was not in the best of moods. By the time the following Sunday rolled around, Mom's courage had returned and she decided that we would once again try church. This time though, Mom was going to sit between the two of us, thinking that would help prevent Greg and me from looking at one another and giggling that eventually turned to loud laughter. I don't know why but back at that age all Greg or I ever had to do was to look at one another and then smile. After that it was all over.

On the third Sunday, Dad had to reschedule his chores on the farm so he too could join us in church. Mom was sure that having a strict father and herself sitting between Greg and me would solve all problems. Mom felt confident that she had everything covered, unfortunately there was no way she could have factored in what was going to happen. By the time the third Sunday arrived, winter had turned cruel and hit us with a Arctic cold blast that just wouldn't quit. The temperatures had dropped well below the zero mark and the inside of the church wasn't much warmer. Luckily, for Greg and me, Mom always bought clothes that were at least three sizes too big, using the theory that eventually we would grow into them. Getting ready for church that morning, under strict orders from Mom, both Greg and I doubled up our clothing with a second pair of shorts, long johns, shirts and even an extra pair of socks.

We must have arrived late for church that Sunday because we had to sit towards the front of the church. Greg had to slide into the pew first followed by Mom then Dad and I was seated on the outside, near the center aisle. Everything was fine until we were about half way through the service. That was when Greg informed Mom that he had to take a leak. The next thing I knew I was nominated to take Greg downstairs to the bathroom. Later Mom did admit that she thought it was taking us way too long and began to worry that maybe Greg and I were getting into something. Mom said the thought that she might have made a mistake asking me to take Greg instead of having Dad do it, began to consume her thoughts. Moments after that thought entered Mom's mind she sighed a breath of relief as she caught a glimpse of Greg and me walking down the aisle. A long silent prayer had just started so Dad stood up and stepped into the aisle, as quietly as he could, followed by Mom. As soon as Mom was standing next to me I blurted out, in a loud voice, "Greg couldn't find his P****." Greg just shrugged his shoulders and slid to his place in the pew. Mom looked towards the heavens and went back to praying.

Mom

While I was writing the Going To Church story, I began to realize all the things Greg and I did to mom not realizing we were, at times, causing her unbearable grief. As you will see, a good share of the time  Greg or I thought we had just found what we considered an excellent solution to a problem, not meaning to irritate Mom. All the other times we were just being boys. I have included a picture of Greg and me with our Mother taken about the time of these memories. This picture was snapped just as we were taking off to see a circus in Boston, a gift given to all of us from our Grandmother on our Mother's side.

The first memory I would like to share with you is a story Mom used to like to tell to prove to Greg how difficult he was, even at a very young age. I was so young that I don't even remember this, so Greg must have been very young.

I think right now would be a good moment to introduce the Foss family. I am sure members of the Foss family will appear in future stories. As far back as I can remember my parent's closest friends were Frank and Evelyn Foss. My first memory of Frank and Evie, as everyone called Evelyn, was when they lived in Peacham. The Foss family moved away by the time I was in fourth grade but they continued to be one of my parent's closest friends. Frank and Evie had two daughters, one a year younger than I was and one a year younger than Greg. Later on in life Frank and Evie had a son which was a year older than my youngest brother Dean and then they had two more daughters. The story I am about to share with you happened when there was just the four of us kids.

We, meaning Greg, Mom and myself, were with Evie and her two daughters in the town of Barton. All of us were in the Foss family car and had driven to Barton, a town about an hour north of Peacham, to visit Frank's parents. From what Mom said Greg was being himself and acting up and knowing Greg, he was probably passing gas too. Mom kept after Greg to straighten out but of course he didn't. Finally Mom told Greg that if he didn't start to behave she would have Evie stop the car and he would have to get out and walk home. A few minutes later the car came to a stop, Mom got out and opened Greg's door. Greg climbed out and headed down the road. At that point Mom started to yell at Greg to come back but Greg kept on walking. Mom finally had to run him down and drag him back to the car.

During my youth I used to chew gum all the time or at least whenever we had any. We were not poor but my parents did not have a lot of extra money either so gum was a considered a treat. Needless to say I would make a stick of gum last all day if possible. Come dinner time I would have to find a place to store my gum until we were finished eating. I got in the habit of spitting my gum in my glass of milk, something I had seen my grandfather do countless times, and then when the milk was gone I would retrieve the gum. Well once in a while I would be so anxious to get back outside to play that I would forget about the gum. Mom would clear the table off and put all of the dishes in the sink full of hot dish water. The next thing Mom knew there would be melted gum over all the dishes. I can't even begin to tell you how many times I caught hell for this.

Also during this period of time Greg and I would go fishing in the brook, at the foot of the hill we lived on, every day. Every morning you would find Greg and me digging worms in the garden and putting them in an old coffee can. After we had what we considered enough worms, we would take off with our fish poles in hand. A couple of times, on the walk to the brook, we would convince ourselves that this was going to be that day that the really big fish would bite. The closer we got to the stream the faster we would walk which would soon be a trot and finally break into a run. Finally, after we were standing in front of a favorite fishing hole, we would reach into the can only to discover we had bounced all the worms out. Another favorite trick we had was to set the can down and not ever find it again or we would knock the can over and not know it until all the worms and made it to safety. So to solve this problem Greg and I used to fill our pants pockets with worms. This worked fine except, by the end of the day, we usually forgot about the worms. A day or so later Mom would do the laundry and when she pulled the clean clothes out of the washer she would find the washing machine full of worms. Even though the worms were really clean by the time mom found them it still upset her.

I also remember walking home from school one very hot afternoon, when I was in seventh grade, and finding a huge frog that had been run over countless times by cars. This frog was as flat as a piece of paper and it had been baked dry in the sun. One corner of the frog had started to curl up so I was able to peel him off the road, whole. In my hand I had the most perfect flat dried frog I had ever seen. I wasn't sure what I was going to do with him but I knew I had to have him. If nothing else I would have the coolest book mark of anyone in school, so I stuck him in my back pocket for safe keeping. Of course, by the time I got home, I had forgotten all about the frog. The next person to see this frog was mom when she was taking the clothes out of the washer and stuck to a pair of pants was this slimy flat frog. That too upset her.

    Then one Sunday morning Greg and I were walking down the hill carrying our poles when we met Alan, a friend of ours, walking towards the village in his Sunday school clothes. Alan didn't think it was right that Greg and I could go fishing while he had to go to Sunday school. So Alan decided to watch us fish until Sunday school was over then he would rush home, change his clothes and join us. Everything worked according to plan until it was time for Alan to run back home. To do this Alan had to cross the brook which was no big deal because there was an old tree that had fallen down and laid across the brook. So all Alan had to do was walk across the old log. We liked this old log because it dammed the water up behind it and as the water flowed over the top of the log it had made a big pool on the lower side. Both spots were excellent for fishing. Greg and I watched as Alan tried to cross the log. Everything went fine until he was about half way across. That is when his slippery Sunday school shoes lost traction. Alan's feet were moving a hundred miles an hour until he finally lost it and fell backwards into the large pool of water on the lower side. Alan landed on his back and his legs were hooked around the top of the log. For a few brief moments Alan did the back stroke while his dress coat floated in the water behind him. Finally Alan just flopped his legs up and fell completely in the water. He then turned to Greg and me, as he waded out of the brook and said, "I probably won't be back."

This last story didn't have a thing to do with our Mom but I wanted to let the reader know Greg and I were not the only boys in town that challenged our Mom's sanity.

Today's Child

Dear Readers,

Up until now I have written stories about my youth and the things that I and my brother got into, sometimes with a little help from our friends, as we traveled through our childhood. Today though, I would like to share with you a very special Father's Day that I spent with one of my granddaughters, Bryana, and the gift she gave me. A gift that cannot be unwrapped and passed around to be looked at but a gift that only the innocence that a four and a half year old could give.

Our house started to fill up two weeks before Father's Day when all of my four daughters came home, one at a time, to be with their sister, Stephanie, Bryana's mom, when she got married. By the time all of my girls arrived along with their children our house was busting at the seams with people and overflowing with noise but it was a good noise. And all of the grandchildren had a blast being together, something that very seldom happens. On Sunday morning, Father's Day, my oldest daughter loaded her van with her four children and headed out on her long trip home. After Angie took off all that was left at our house was Bryana and her parents Stephanie and Nick.

By the time the noon hour had arrived Nick and Steph's Jeep and trailer were loaded and they were ready to begin their journey to the west coast to start a life for themselves. The plan was for Steph and Nick to make the trip alone, along with the cat that is, to Washington state, Bryana would stay with us for two weeks. We would then fly out with Bryana and hopefully in those two weeks Steph and Nick would have had time to make the drive and get their home ready.

Soon after Steph and Nick took off for Washington, I headed for the couch to try to get in a short nap. The previous two weeks had taken its toll on me. It did not take Bryana long to find me and as soon as she did she was after me to take her to camp so she could go swimming. The camp Bryana wanted to go to is the camp that my parents built in the early 60's. That camp is still in our family, owned by my two brothers and myself.

Finally at 4:00 I had to give in to Bryana. We grabbed Bryana's swimming suit and a towel, jumped into my pickup and headed to camp. When we got to camp we were greeted by a cold strong wind but that didn't seem to matter to a four year old and Bryana didn't waste any time in putting her suit on and jumping into the water. I sat on the pontoon boat watching Bryana until I saw her chin start to chatter so much that her teeth were clanging together. I spoke up and made the suggestion that we should go home. Bryana must have been cold because she didn't argue at all.

On our trip home, Bryana, like she normally is, was full of questions, some I of which I had answered countless times before. And like the many trips we had made earlier this year, when we drove past the farm that was spreading manure, I told Bryana that

she should be ashamed of herself and she should say sorry. Again she slapped herself in the forehead and dragged her hand down across her face and said in a loud irritated voice, "Gampa, I told you it is the cows."

Soon after the farm we had to drive up a very steep hill, Cemetery Hill. At the top of the hill is a pure white fence and just beyond this fence are all of the grave stones, some aged by the weather and others that are new. As we drove slowly past the cemetery I asked Bryana if she would like to see where my mom and dad were buried. Much to my surprise Bryana said, "yes, I would like to see Gram and Papa". I pulled my truck along side of the white fence and parked it. I stepped out of the driver's door and started to walk towards the open fence. By the time I reached the back of my truck Bryana was just rounding the corner of the truck running as fast as she could. Together we walked side by side through the open gate and down the paved path until we came to the first turn. At this turn I stepped onto the grass between two very old head stones and started walking towards my parent's stone. Bryana reached up with her small hand and placed it in mine. Bryana and I walked slowly past all of the stones that had stood for countless years, some even had moss growing on them. I was aware that Bryana was talking but by then my mind had started to wander and I was wondering why Bryana, all of a sudden, had a need to see her great grandparent's grave. Bryana never knew either of my parents. My mom had died two years before Bryana was born and even though my dad had a chance to hold his great granddaughter once, she was only about a month old. I then realized that Bryana probably felt she knew her great grandparent's through the memories of her mom and aunts.

 Moments later Bryana and I were standing in front of my parent's grave. I pointed to their stone and said to her, "This is where my parents live now." Bryana asked me if they would ever move from here and I said, "No they will be here forever and ever" Bryana then spoke up and said, "Leave" Not being sure of what I thought I had heard I said, "What?" Bryana said, " Gampa please leave, I have something I want to say to Gram and Papa." With that I started to walk off slowly reading the names on the stones as I passed them. When I was three to four stones away I looked back at Bryana. Bryana was bent over kissing the names on my parent's stone of granite. A lump came to my throat but I was able to find my voice and I asked Bryana if I could come back? Bryana said, "NO".

So I kept on walking and reading. About ten minutes later I hear this little voice yell out, "Gampa." I said, "I'll be right there." I had taken just a few steps when I could once again see her. From where I was standing it looked like Bryana was digging in the flowers that were in front of my parent's grave. It was on the tip of my tongue to say something but something inside of me told me to wait. Moments later I was standing beside Bryana and my eyes watched as she tried to plant the wild flowers she had found. Fighting back tears I said to Bryana that it was time to leave.

As Bryana and I walked side by side towards the paved path the questions once again flowed freely out of her., "Why is that stone so high and pointed? Why is that stone black? Look Gampa that stone has a picture on it. Why does that grave look like a tree?" And so on and so on. By the time we were at the top of the path, where it turned towards the open gate, the place where earlier we had stepped onto the grass Bryana asked me if there was someone buried under each stone? I said, "Yes there is." With that Bryana placed her hand in mine and we walked through the open gate. The moment we were standing outside the fence I knew that behind me/us were all of the fading faces of yesterday's children and in my hand was today's child.

Bye Peanut

I knew the last two weeks that Bryana (aka Peanut and sometimes Bug A Boo) stayed with us would go fast, I just didn't realize that time could travel at the speed that it did. Those fourteen days went by so fast that they are now just a blur in days gone by, but the memories Bryana left with me will live for all of the days that are yet to come.

The first few days were rather calm ones, but looking back I think Bryana was just resting up from all of the excitement of the wedding and having her cousins around to play with from morning until night. About Tuesday of the first week the old Bryana  started to show herself again. I know she is only four and a half but in those few years Bryana has learned much about being a kid. She loves to hide things, especially if she thinks you might need them in a hurry, play tricks on you, some of which are evil and she is a master of ambush. If you don't believe me just ask the dog.

One evening we were all watching TV when a commercial came on. I decided I would run to the kitchen and grab a snack. To get to the kitchen all that I had to do was walk the length of the coffee table. Then between coffee table and a love seat, through the dining room then into the kitchen. As soon as I stood up from the couch and rounded the coffee table Peanut jumped from her chair and tackled me from behind. She wrapped both of her legs around one of mine and was hanging off my belt holding on with both of her hands. This made walking very difficult but not impossible. By the time I got to the end of the coffee table where I had to walk between the table and love seat my pants had started to creep down. Bryana then put one foot against the love seat and somehow she got her other foot on the back of my slipper and stomped down. I hate to admit it but I couldn't move and Bryana showed no interest in letting go. I was finally able to turn enough so I could reach

the back of her pants and I gave her a wedgie. When she reached back to dig her shorts out of her back side I was able to break free.

The rest of the first week was full of Bryana doing her normal daily things to me, like locking me out of the bathroom, stealing my clothes or beating everyone to the phone. The moment that phone rang you would hear Bryana's feet hit the floor and she was off running, yelling I'll get it, I'll get it. Once in a while it would be a telemarketer and listening to Peanut's questions was a riot. It would usually start off with, "Well who is this?, " No Mom is not here but Nana is, who are you? No, I asked you first. Then I would hear Bryana hang up the phone. I would ask her who it was. Bryana's reply, " I don't know they hung up on me."

At the end of the first week I had to be away Saturday and part of Sunday to help an old friend. Late Sunday afternoon, when I got home, Peanut met me at the door and within the first five minutes she had run off with my gym bag, dumped everything on the bedroom floor, stole my belt, hid it and locked me out of the bathroom, twice. This seemed to quench her need to, "pick on me", because the rest of the night went without incident.

The last week was filled with a going away party at Bryana's day care, spending a night with a friend and spending a day with her aunt on her dad's side of the family Towards the end of the week, even though Bryana tried not to show any emotion and claimed that it wouldn't bother her leaving us, you could tell that it was beginning to weigh heavy on her. Bryana is a lot like her mother that way.

Saturday afternoon we drove down to Ct. to spend the night with a daughter of ours. As it turned out Alison was going to be the one to fly Bryana out to Washington state. Sunday morning, after breakfast, we finished packing and got ready to leave. During these last goodbyes Bryana started to break down and cry. She did however keep it together enough to climb on the back of the chair I was sitting in and crawl up onto to my shoulders and want to go for a piggy back ride. We walked around the room a few times but by then it was time to leave. Carrying arm loads of luggage we made our way to the cars. Alison's car was right in front of her apartment and our car in the parking lot. Alison and Bryana walked us to our car, helping to carry a few things. When we hugged Bryana and gave her a kiss her flood gates opened and the tears ran down her cheeks as did ours. Alison finally took Bryana by the hand and started to walk back towards her car. I backed our car out from its

parking space and drove to the exit. I stopped to look both ways and all I could hear was a little girl crying, a big bush between our car and Alison's hid Bryana from our view. I couldn't stand it another second, I put the car in park and both Nana and I walked to Alison's car to get in one last bye. That good bye was no easier than any of the others but at least we got one more glimpse of Peanut.

As we drove towards the interstate we decided to stop at Dunkin Donuts to grab a coffee and a donut to take with us on the long trip home. A couple of  minutes after Nana went inside to grab our snacks a familiar looking car pulled in beside mine. The back window of that car rolled down and Bryana was looking out at me. Alison said Bryana wanted us to follow them to the airport exit so she could wave good bye to us one last time. When Nana came out of Dunkin Donuts she didn't recognize the back of Alison's car and wanted to know who I was talking to. I just leaned back so she could see for herself.

For the next fifteen to twenty minutes we followed Alison but when the airport exit got near I pulled alongside of Alison's car and we waved good bye. Later Alison told us that Bryana was fine until she pulled off the highway and our tail lights slowly disappeared in the traffic. That, according to Alison, was when Bryana completely lost it ...

.......Goodbye Peanut......I miss you, already.

Stay Away From the Brook

One early spring Greg and I found an uncontrollable need to be near the brook when the ice was breaking up. This fascination of watching ice float down stream was also shared by one of our neighbors and close friend, Alan. Alan had earned the nick name, Anything Alan, because he was always up to doing anything that came to his mind or anyone else's mind, for that matter. The three of us decided that we would meet by the bridge, Saturday morning, at the foot of the hill that Greg and I lived on.

Right after breakfast Saturday morning, Greg and I dressed up and headed out the door. The last thing we heard was mom yell out, "Don't go near the brook", which we both had to promise to. Fortunately for us, Greg's and my theory on a promise is it wasn't really broken unless we got caught. A theory shared by most kids back then.

In Alan's excitement he took off early so we met half way up our hill instead of at the foot of the hill. After a short discussion we decided to cut across the big field and head towards a calm section of the brook. The field had only scattered patches of snow left on it so the walking was fairly easy and fast. A few minutes later we stood on the bank of the brook and we couldn't believe how big it looked, especially considering we had to be on the other side. I should probably mention now, that this brook has shrunk considerable over the years. Back when we were kids this brook was only slightly smaller than the Mississippi, but now it has shrunk to only the size of a small brook. I think our water table has gone down a lot since those earlier years or something.

 I think I was the one that came up with the bright idea that we could probably run across on the ice that was left on the brook. Alan wasn't really sure about that so he thought I should be the first one to try it. I took a couple of deep breaths and took off on a dead run going as fast as my legs would carry me. In one section I could hear the ice cracking pretty bad but I kept on going and less than a second later I was safe on the other side. Seconds later Alan was standing beside me and said, "Wow, did you hear that ice cracking as I ran across?"   About the time Alan said, "Wow" Greg was in the middle of this run when a big section of ice broke free. Greg dropped to his knees and grabbed onto the edge of the ice and he started to float down stream. Moments later Greg, still on his hands and knees holding onto the edge of the ice with eyes as big as silver dollars, went out of sight as the brook rounded a corner. Alan, looked at me, shrugged his shoulder and said, "We better head up stream to the beaver dam to see if the ice is safe there."

Ten or maybe fifteen minutes later Greg came trudging up through the snow and he looked a little mad. Alan and I were sliding across the ice that was still on the beaver dam. Greg's mood seemed to lighten up a bit when Alan finally asked him how far he got. Greg said it was really scary and he got all the way down to where the brook goes into the woods. A smile then came over Greg's face and he came flying off the bank and slid across the ice on his belly.

Fridays With Mom

In Loving Memory Of Our Mother
March 12, 1931 – July 26, 2005

One of mom's jobs was to do the weekly shopping, a chore mom soon learned to dread. From the stories that mom used to tell us, things started to go bad for her early on, in fact soon after she had Greg potty trained, another chore that tested every fiber of her being. I am afraid that story must stay within the confines of the family though.

The first little incident happened on a busy Friday afternoon on Railroad Street, the business district of St. Johnsbury, Vt. On this particular day mom had to go to the hardware store to pick something up for dad. On Railroad Street there was a hardware store called the Peck Co. This was a very large store that had everything possible under the sun inside its four walls and the front of the store was as impressive as was all of its merchandise inside. To enter the store you had to walk through two big swinging glass doors which had a big display case on both sides. On one side there was a kitchen set up with a stove, sink, refrigerator and overhead lights above a dining room table. On the other side of the door there was a bathroom, complete with a tub, shower, a sink in front of a large mirror surrounded by lights and a toilet off to one side. From what mom said the day went without incident until she got to the checkout counter and had to let go of Greg's hand for a few minutes. By the time mom had opened her purse, paid the bill and put her change away, the space that Greg used to occupy was empty. So mom started her search, which in a short time turned frantic. That is until she looked towards the front of the store and notice a kid standing in front of the toilet with his pants down to his knees. Dad always said that for those few moments, the people walking by the store, probably figured it was a very realistic display.

The next little incident happened in the W.T. Grants store which was also on Railroad Street. I won't mention any names here but like before mom had to take us boys shopping with her and like before one of us got away from her. Again mom started her search, hoping that the missing child was still in the store and much to her disappointment he was. She found the missing son crawling around on the floor looking up ladies dresses.

The final straw also happened in W.T. Grants. Mom got distracted for just a few short moments and Greg got away. Mom's search took her around the store twice before she finally found him. This time

Greg was in the women's apparel department feeling up one of the mannequins that was displaying bras.

After the bra episode mom refused to take Greg and me shopping with her. It then became a Friday night event, that way mom could go shopping alone while Greg and I sat in the car with dad. I can remember sitting in the car in the parking lot of the old A&P store with dad and watching mom as she got out of the car and ran for the safety of the store. Dad would start in, with what turned out to be his weekly speech, "I think your mom is going to run away from home.", "And the way you two act I can't blame her." After a few minutes of silence and deep thought Greg finally ask if that meant we could have hot dogs every night for dinner.

May you rest in peace Mom,
you have earned it.

Trigger

One nice summer evening, after the dinner dishes were washed and put away, my parents decided it was time for us to visit my dad's aunt and uncle that lived in E. Peacham. Just as we were pulling into the dooryard cousin Bill came from the opposite direction riding his horse, Trigger. Bill was five years older than I was and I always envied him because he seemed to have so much fun riding his horse, which he was always riding bareback. As usual the second we got out of the car I was hounding Bill to let me ride his horse. While Bill was trying to talk me out of riding the horse a pickup pulled into the driveway. It was Alan, just getting home from his construction job.

Alan was the oldest of a family of three boys and one girl with Bill being the youngest. My first memory of Alan was the summer he got out of the navy. Alan had joined the navy when he was only seventeen and I was too young to remember him before that. Soon after Alan returned from the service my parents stopped at Alan's parents to visit him. When we pulled into the dooryard I noticed a ladder leaning against the house and someone was on the roof painting. Well that person was Alan and he was covered all over his upper body with paint. A smile came over my face because there, on the roof, was an adult that painted just like I did. Only later did I find out that while Alan was in the navy he got covered with something called tattoos.

Well much to my delight Alan stood up for me and told Bill that he was sure I was old enough to ride the horse. Bill hesitated for a moment but finally made a cup with his hands, I place one foot in his hands and swung one leg over the back of the horse while Bill hoisted me up. Less than a second later I was sitting on top of this horse and I couldn't believe how far down the ground looked. As it turned out I had this false sense of security sitting on this big horse.

For the next minute or so I sat jigging up and down, with my legs sticking straight out on the wide back of the horse, saying giddy up but the horse didn't budge an inch. Finally Bill or Alan, I don't remember which one said, , "You'll have to dig your heals into her side." I lifted both legs as high as I could and drove them into the side of the horse. By the time my hat hit the ground we were already at the far end of the field. That is the spot where the field makes a very steep drop off to the brook below. As we shot across the field I remember bounding up and down on the back of the horse and pulling back on the reins as far as I could but I was so small that I couldn't even take the slack out of the reins.

Whenever Bill rode the horse she always plodded along and in a single swaying movement Bill and the horse came up the road, just as calm and graceful as a butterfly floating in the air. I was not on the horse very long but I sure remember how uncomfortable it was pounding up and down on the back bone of the horse. For a brief moment I thought I was riding a jack hammer. When we got to the end of the field the horse came to an abrupt halt and dropped her front end. I shot off the back of the horse much like a stunt man is shot out of a cannon at the circus, except I didn't have a net to land on. I never touched ground again until I was about 3/4 of the way down the steep bank. When I hit it knocked most of the wind out of me. The next two flops I took, before coming to a rest on top of bed of rocks, finished taking the rest of the air out of me.

I laid where I landed for a few minutes, changing colors as I tried to breath, all the time wondering if I would ever walk again. After what seemed like eternity, I crawled up the steep bank and walked back to the barn. The horse had beaten me back by a good ten minutes. Bill, Alan and my brother Greg were still laughing and I swear the horse was wearing a smile....You would have thought that would have cured my desire to ride but as it turned out I had many more disappointments waiting for me. Not only with horses but I didn't have any better luck trying to ride a goat, pig and even a bicycle at times.

Hard Cider

During my sophomore year at Peacham Academy, I was fortunate enough to become really good friends with Burt. Burt was a year older than I was and had his driver's license. Having a driver's license was great only if you had a car, which Burt didn't have. But he was able to borrow his mother's cars on several occasions. And on a few of those occasions, when Burt dropped me off at my house, we would have to take the time to find a big hammer and a block of wood and try our luck at knocking some of the fresh dents out of his mom's car. Once in a while my dad would even help us, probably thankful that it wasn't his car.

I had met Burt two years before when he first entered P.A. as an eighth grader but we never became friends until our freshman year, the year Burt got his drivers permit. I was lucky enough to be with Burt several times when his mom, younger brother and he made the trip to Barre to visit his grandmother. We really love this trip because it gave Burt a chance to practice his driving and at that age driving is almost everything. The only thing better than driving was getting a chance to drive fast. Burt's mom was a very hard working lady and would fall asleep the moment she had a chance to sit still for a few minutes. Usually fifteen minutes in the car would do it. The moment Burt's mom nodded off Burt would start picking speed up. Forty plus years later I can still hear the screams when Burt's mom would wake up. I also learned a few really good cuss words.

Burt, having his driving license, did however present us with a problem we hadn't counted on. All we wanted to do after school was to drive around, but Burt's mom got real sick of paying for the gas so that activity came to a immediate halt. With this new problem staring both Burt and I in the face we tried to come up with something we could do to make money that involved driving. After a while we decided that making and selling cider would do it for us. It was a hard sell but we finally convinced Burt's mom to supply us with gas money until the cash started to roll in from all the cider we would sell.

The next afternoon, after school, Burt and I gathered up some old grain sacks and went to every apple orchard we could find. I don't know how many bags of apples we picked but the trunk of the car was full as was the back seat. The next day we were going to drive to the nearby town of Topsham, to a place that had a huge cider press. Before we took off someone, luckily, pointed out that we would need jugs to put the cider in. So instead of getting the apples pressed that day we spent the afternoon going house to house begging for old gallon jugs. A few days later we were back at the same houses selling the jugs back to them, only this time filled with cider.

Again we had to postpone our trip to the cider press because someone else pointed out that we might want to think about washing these old jugs first, yet wasting more of our valuable time. As it turned out, that was good advice, especially after seeing what was in some of the jugs. Finally after three days we were ready to make the trip to Topsham. Burt and I got about two miles out of Peacham when a dog ran out in front of us and again we were off the road. Now not only did we have to get the apples pressed into cider but we also had to find the time to dig the hammer and 2 by 4 out and do a little more body work.

On the trip back home, Burt and I decided that after we had paid his mom back, we would take what was left over, our profit, and buy some boxing gloves. It wasn't long before I started to call them hitting gloves, you would not believe how fast Burt's left was. I did however get even with Burt by beating all the protective covering off his left glove with my face, but that is another story for another time.

Much to our surprise, even after we bought the hitting gloves, we had a few dollars left. By then both Burt and I had the taste of being, in our eyes, successful business men. That is when we came up with the idea of taking what was left of our cider money, buying some raisins, yeast and sugar. We would then take the few gallons of cider we had left and make it hard. After the cider got done fermenting and good and hard we would sell it to the dorm students and make another killing. Another killing did come but not as we had planned.

Burt and I had cleaned out a spot in his closet and put the cider in there for safe keeping. Every day, after school, we would run to his room and watch the bubbles escape from the hose we had coming out of each gallon jug which was submerged in a big pan full of water. After about two weeks of waiting we couldn't take it anymore and decided that we owed it to ourselves to have the first drink. Burt's mom had to work late that night so we both poured a big glass and had a sip. It was awful but still we drank it, figuring sooner or later, we would acquire a taste for our hard cider. We were wrong. After about two glass neither Burt or I could take any more. Something must have gone wrong because it was three days before either Burt or I could be away from the bathroom long enough to go back to school.

As hard as this was on us, we decided we got away easy. God only knows what would have happened to us if we had sold some of this cider to the dorm students. Some of the dorm boys were pretty big. Burt and I hid the rest of the cider in the science building of Peacham Academy and as far as I know it is still there.

Spelling

Memories from the first couple years of school are few in number. My mom however had one that she used to tell every chance that came along. My parents, just a short time before my first day of school, had purchased an 8mm movie camera. On the morning of my first day of first grade, mom had the camera ready and took pictures of a kid running for all he was worth, with a new Lone Ranger lunch box swinging in one hand wearing a new fall jacket, out the dooryard for the bus. In the next shot you see this very disgusted looking kid get off the school bus, walking very slowly toward the house dragging his new jacket on the ground behind him and the hand holding the lunch box was limp. Later, mom said as she looked through the movie camera lens, that she knew the next twelve years were going to be long ones.

As I said earlier I don't have many memories from the first few years of school but one that has stuck with me all these years is the evil way our teacher used to try to shame all of us kids into learning our spelling. Every week we had to take a spelling test and each word we got wrong we had to sit at our desk and write it until we had learned how to spell it. Then to make matters worse, each of us were called up to the teacher's desk, one at a time, and we had to spell each of our wrong words out loud for the teacher as she called them off. Taters (I don't know if nicknames are common now, but back then they sure were. Besides Taters we had Duffer, Rat Eye, Gorilla, Stink and Thumper just to mention a few.) was being tortured in front of the class when a piece of paper fell off the teachers desk. Mrs. Carpenter, a very large and wide woman, rolled up on one side to reach the piece of paper on the floor and she must have strained herself pretty bad to sit back up because this really loud long blast of air shot out her back side, right at Taters....I swear that the whole world quit making noise at that very moment. I mean it was so quiet that there was a house fly on the window sill that coughed and we all heard it. Within a half a second all of us kids had our hands pinching our noises and covering our mouths trying not to laugh. And Taters, with his back towards us, was all alone standing in front of the class. Almost instantly his ears turned a bright red and you could see his back start to shake as he too tried not to laugh. After a few agonizing seconds, Taters turned to face the class and it was all over for all of us. I don't remember the exact words that came out of Mrs. Carpenter but all of us kids got yelled at for laughing. Taters never did finish spelling his words and the next few kids that were singled out got laughing so hard they too were sent back to their seats.

I also remember getting on the school bus one morning and having to sit by a girl that looked to be almost as old as my mom. I finally got up the nerve to ask her what grade she was in. She told me, "Junior". I then asked her what number that would be and she said eleven. I remember thinking I had just turned six and she had been in school longer than I had been alive. I then wondered what I had gotten myself into this time................As it turned out mom was right, it was a long twelve years.

On All Fours

Even though my brother, Greg, and I never started to work full time on the poultry farm until the summer of 1962, we spent a lot of time there with our dad and grandfather. We spent most of our time getting in the way, the rest of the time we kept ourselves busy stepping on ants, throwing stones and bothering the chickens.

One day Greg was at the farm playing outside one of the hen houses while dad and pup were busy building a new grain bin. At one point Greg started to scream and yell a lot. At the time Greg was well known for yelling and screaming a lot when he even thought he might have hurt himself. So every time Greg yelled dad would holler back, "I'll be right up, in the mean time be quiet, you'll scare the chickens." Later dad had to admit that he wasn't sure how long it was before he checked on Greg and said he felt real bad when he saw what Greg had done to himself. Greg had jumped onto a board and drove five nails into his foot. Greg couldn't get his foot off the board and he even went as far as unlacing his sneakers but it didn't seem to matter how hard he pulled on his leg his foot stuck tight to the board.

Dad took Greg home and mom decided he better go to the doctor, who by then knew both Greg and me by first name, to get the holes cleaned out. Then mom said to Greg, "You'll probably need a tetanus shot." When I heard mom say that, I spoke up and said, "Hold on a minute, if Greg has to get a shot I want to see it, it's probably gonna make him yell." As it turned out Greg did have to have a tetanus shot but things backfired on me in the end. When Greg was done with his shot the doctor said, "Well as long as Gary is here he might as well get a tetanus shot too because I am sure he'll need one before the summer is over."

When we got home Greg said to me as I walked to the laundry room door, "would you mind waiting a minute and hold the door for me?" When I turned around Greg was coming across the garage floor on all fours. I said, "What are you doing?", "Well", Greg said, "It hurts to walk on my foot." I no longer remember how long Greg creeped on all fours but it used to irritate Dave and me to no end because we were always having to wait for Greg to catch up. It got to be a real pain to walk to the village store which was almost a half a mile away. It didn't seem to matter how slow Dave and I walked we still had to make frequent stops to wait for Greg. I can still remember seeing Greg crawling up the stairs to the store porch and how we had to hold the door for him. Then once in the store if Greg wanted something that was more than a foot off the floor Dave or I had to get it for him. I can just imagine what strangers, driving by, must have thought when they saw this poor five to six year old boy on all fours trying his best to keep up with a couple of bigger kids.

After a while Greg wore holes, not only in his pants, but also his knees and it ended up hurting him more to creep than to walk so finally he went back to walking upright.

The Old Car Trunk Lid

One snowy afternoon, after school that is, a bunch of us boys were sitting around trying to come up with a new and faster sled, something that would take us down the hills of Peacham really fast and put some excitement back into our lives. I think it was John B that first spoke up with his idea. John B was a natural born inventor. John could take common everyday items and come up with a new use for them in a moment's notice. John also had the ability to see things that needed to be invented and he had the ingenuity to follow through with his ideas. Fortunately none of his inventions ever caught on because in the end all John was ever good at inventing was a new and quicker way of getting hurt. One of his best known disasters was the bicycle built for two. John took two bikes, removed the front wheel of one, loosened the bolts that held the rear wheel on the other one and then slid the front fork over the rear axle bolts of the second bike. Neither bike, of course, had anything that resembled a brake. The next time I saw that bike it was in pieces and John, all bruised with big scabs everywhere, refused to talk about it.

Well it was John that came up with the brilliant idea of taking an old car trunk lid and using that for a sled and he knew where there was one. A few years earlier John's home on Ha Penny had burned to the ground and his family had bought a house in the village on the hill between Peacham and E. Peacham. John claimed there were a few old cars in the woods near their old house and all we had to do was take the hood we wanted. On the following Saturday John and I borrowed a few of our father's wrenches, without their permission, (our dads had already learned not to lend any of their tools to us, especially if they ever wanted to see them again) and headed for the old cars. Just like John had said, there were about four cars to choose from. We settled on a late 30's or early 40's car that had the trunk lid that curved down, we figured it would be a comfortable fit.

The lid came off much easier than we had planned on but we never had any idea it would be as heavy as it was. I'll bet it weighed close to 80 pounds. It was heavy. Then to make matters worse we never thought to bring along any rope to tie to it so we could drag it to the village which was about two miles away. It seemed like it took the two us almost forever being bent over pushing the lid but we finally made it.

There was a big sliding party planned for Saturday night on the steep hill that went from Peacham Village to E. Peacham. This was the hill that John lived on. Both John and I knew that we would be the envy of everyone there as soon as we hauled the trunk lid out. So with that in mind, we kept this a secret, knowing some of the other boys would probably want to try it out first as soon as they heard about it.

    At about 7:00 pm the hill was full of kids sliding and a light snow had started to fall which made the hill very fast. It was about that time that John and I pulled out our secret sled from its hiding place. After a lot of tugging and pulling we had the trunk lid at the top of the hill. Much to our surprise not a single kid showed any interest in being the first one to try this out, in fact many just stood off in a distance. John and I both got in the trunk lid each of us taking a side and with a few pushes with our hands we were off. Moments later I began to think I might have made a mistake getting into this trunk lid. Right after we took off this lid started to spin as fast as any sit 'n' spin I had ever seen and we were picking up speed at an alarming rate. I guess with the weight of the trunk and two kids this shouldn't have surprised me though. As we went spinning down the hill I happened to notice one of John's brothers on top of a snow bank, which was about eight to ten feet high, in front of their house. The next time around I noticed that Daniel had a tricycle on top of the snow bank and he was getting ready to ride it down the snow bank. The next time around Daniel was about half way down the bank. The next time I saw Daniel, he was right in front of us, his eyes were wide open with the look of death in them….. John too had seen his brother riding the tricycle down the snow bank and put both of his feet out to push the bike and Daniel out of the way. The next time Daniel should have come into my vision all I saw a tricycle sitting there and Daniel was nowhere to be seen. John had missed the tricycle and hit Daniel in the chest with his feet and cleaned him right off the tricycle…….By the time John and I had dragged the trunk back up the hill John's dad was waiting for us. At his suggestion and out of the fear of our lives we put the trunk away forever……. I am happy to say that Daniel survived that ordeal and many more.

The Brooding House

Sometime during the late 50's or early 60's my grandparents bought a big old building in the small town of West Burke Vt. and converted it to a brooding house. This big old three story building, in its former life, was a small A&W Root Beer factory. Now it was where we housed day old chicks and raised them until they started to lay which was about twenty one weeks of age. This building had a really neat elevator which we used to take the birds up to the second and third floors. And when the birds reached laying age, we again used the elevator to take them back out of the building and truck them to the main poultry farm in Peacham. This old elevator was, however, so worn that you had to be sure to load it equally or you would find yourself wedged between two floors. When that happened all you could do was move the crates of birds one at a time and between each crate that you piled in a different corner you would jump on the floor of the elevator. Eventually it would become unstuck and drop until the cable once again became tight. You would then force your heart back down into your chest and continue on your way.

This old building was sandwiched between an old mom and pop country store and a small restaurant and on the third floor there was this really neat one room apartment. This apartment was very small and there was only room for a sink, stove, refrigerator and a dining room table. On one outside wall was a couple of small beds and through a door in one corner was a bathroom. Until the birds, and there were thousands of them, reached a couple of weeks of age someone was with them twenty four hours a day. I used to love to spend nights in that apartment with my dad or grandfather, especially my grandfather. Pup had a sweet tooth and we ate mostly junk food.

After I grew up and found myself remembering those days I often wonder what the owner of the store and the restaurant owners thought about our annual trip to West Burke. Chickens have their own unique smell and to most, if not all, people, not that pleasant of a smell either. If either one of our neighbors ever had a problem they never said a word and were always very nice to both Greg and myself. The owner of the store, I think his name was Mr. Randall, had a hobby of raising fighting cocks and housed those roosters in pens behind his store which was right next to our brooding house. One night, when our chicks were about a month or so old, Mr Randall was awakened in the early morning hours by a loud noise behind his store. Minutes later all went quiet again and Mr. Randall went back to sleep. Mid morning we showed up to feed and care for the young birds when Mr. Randall told us that he wanted to show us something out behind our buildings. We walked, with Mr. Randall, behind the brooding house and it looked like a war zone next to one pens that housed one of the fighting cocks, I mean there were pieces of shirt and blood all over the place. As near as we could figure someone planned on stealing a few of our young birds and accidentally got into the wrong pen.

One year, when we were putting the finishing touches on cleaning up the building after we had shipped the birds to Peacham, dad walked out the back door and onto the loading platform, carrying an arm full of boxes. Evidently he forgot about the hole in the floor and fell through it. I thought for a few minutes that he was going to cry but he didn't. After the fall both Greg and I noticed that dad favored one side and he talked funny and gasped for air a lot. Things went downhill for dad at supper that night and once again I thought he was going to cry.

At our dinner table I always sat across from dad. Part way through the meal, with a lot of effort and noise on dads part, he grabbed his glass of milk and tipped it up to take a drink. I spoke up and told him that I thought he was drinking my milk. Dad asked me how come I thought it was my milk. I said, "because I can see my gum in the bottom of it", back then if I was chewing gum at meal time I would spit my gum in my glass of milk and if I remembered when I finished eating, I would go back to chewing. Well this struck mom funny and she started this high pitched laugh. Dad almost choked on his (my) milk and started to laugh himself, but that hurt him so much that it cut his breathing off and the funny noises once again started to come out of him. This made mom laugh even harder which in turn got dad to laughing even though he couldn't.

    After mom and dad calmed down mom decided that it was time for dad to go to the doctors. We all sat in the car while dad went into the emergency clinic and after what seemed like eternity dad came walking out. He had broken a few ribs. Our next stop was a drug store on main street so dad could buy a huge rib cage bandage to wrap around his chest to help hold his ribs in place. Dad came out of the drug store and threw a small package on the front seat and slid on the passenger seat. I picked the package up and said I didn't think this bandage was going to help much. Dad asked me how come? I said, " because it says wrist on it." That too got mom to laughing and once again dad tried his luck at not laughing, but like the time before all he did was make funny noises.

    I also remember one other time when dad forgot about a hole. This happened on the day of his long egg route. On this particular day dad took off early in the morning with his truck loaded with eggs to deliver to all his customers and for some reason that day didn't go smooth at all. Dad didn't return until early evening and by the time he unloaded his truck and stopped at his parent's house to drop off the sales book and cash, Gramme and Pup had already sat down for dinner. Dad just dropped off all the receipts and stepped out the door and walked around the corner of the house headed towards his car, thinking only about dinner and relaxing in front of the TV. About the time Gramme and Pup sat back down to the dinner table was when they heard the splash. Dad had forgotten that his parents had trouble with their cess pool and the cover was off it. When Pup looked out the window he could see dad was in over his waist and wading towards shore.

Greg the Cobbler

During the late 60's and early 70's there were several dance halls that catered to the teens and kids in their early twenties. For a while, during the last few years of the 60's, the place to be on Saturday night was The Cave. The Cave was in Barton Vt., a town about an hour's drive from my home town of Peacham. The Cave, in its former life, was the barn for a very large dairy farm that, for one reason or another, had ceased to operate. The owners cleaned out the upper part of the barn, which had been the hay mow, built a stage at one end and lined the outside walls with folding chairs. The walls were also laced with every possible color of light. On the stage along with the huge speakers there were a couple of strobe lights and high in the peak of the building were black lights. A hay field next to the building was kept mowed during the summer months and plowed during the winter and was used for parking. There was no way for the owners to mark off parking spaces so you just parked where ever you found a spot, regardless of where it was or who it might have blocked off. This parking lot, itself, was a source of many arguments and fender benders.

I remember one time when my brother Greg, my best friend Albert and I rode up with my cousin Bill. Bill was home on leave from the service and we talked him into taking us up to The Cave, guaranteeing him a night he wouldn't soon forget. As it turned out Bill had many such nights with us, but those stories will have to wait for another time. On the trip to Barton, Albert and I accidentally discovered that Bill had a six pack of beer hidden under the front seat. Albert and I came up with, what we considered an elaborate plan to get the two of us in the car alone with Bill's beer. After we had been at the dance for a while we hunted Bill down and told him that we needed a break from the loud noise and all the smoke that had filled the hall. Bill must have been in a generous mood because he just handed over the keys, either that or he had found a girl he was interested in and wanted Albert and me somewhere else. The first thing Albert and I did was dig the beer out from under the front seat and cracked open a couple of them. Both Albert and I were uncomfortable drinking the beer because we were in plain sight of the policeman that stood by the front door, so we had to time our sips when he was looking the other way. After a few minutes of nervous drinking, the car that was parked on the other side of the car we were parked next to, pulled out and drove off. I figured, as long as I had the key and all I had to do was move one parking spot Bill wouldn't mind, especially if it meant we didn't get caught, by the policeman, drinking Bill's beer. After the beer was gone, Albert and I went back into the dance hall. After a while we bumped into Bill who wanted to know what took us so long. , "Nothing", I said, "Oh by the way you are out of beer and there is a scratch that runs from the front fender, across the driver's door and stops about half way down the back fender, but neither Albert or I thinks it looks all that bad."

We used to take turns driving to The Cave and hopefully your week of driving happened to line up with the week that your car was running, otherwise we had the problem of finding another way to make the trip. One Saturday night when it was my turn to drive, I happened to be the first person to get to my car when the dance was over. I started the engine and put the defroster on trying to clear the windshield enough to see through it. Getting out of the parking lot was, on a good night, a nightmare and all others nights were even worse than that. No sooner had a little hole, just big enough to look through, appeared on my windshield when I noticed an opening in the line of traffic that was heading out. I didn't want to miss my chance and I figured the other guys that rode with me would find me in the line of traffic anyway, so I grabbed this spot. A minute or so later one of the back doors opened and Greg got in mad as hell about something. Come to find out Greg had gotten to the car a few minutes earlier, he knew it was a long ride back home and figured it would be much nicer if he started the trip with an empty bladder. So with that in mind Greg stood behind the car making that all possible. Greg said he looked up and I had driven off leaving him in the middle of the parking lot taking a leak, with all the other car lights on him.

When I started writing this story it was my intention to share with you a little story about Greg and a pair of loafers he had. During this time in Greg's life he was well known for his ability to pinch every penny he ever had in his hands, until it screamed, and then stretch it to its limits. Greg had a pair of loafers that he had become particularly attached to. These loafers were the type that were stitched around the top of the foot and these loafers were in pretty good shape, or at least according to Greg, except the stitching had started to come apart. After supper, one night, Greg got up from the dinner table and walked out the laundry door and into the garage. A few minutes later Greg returned and in one hand was a large snarl of old fishing line. Greg sat down and started to unsnarl the line until he thought there was enough there to stitch the top of his loafers. He then dug around in Mom's sewing basket until he found a large old needle, one with an eye big enough to thread fishing line through. Greg then grabbed the one bad shoe and started working on it. After a while Greg held this shoe up and with an approving grin looked over his work. Greg was so impressed with his new found ability that he stitched the other shoe using the theory that it would need it sooner or later anyways.

    That Saturday night, as with all the previous Saturday nights, found us at The Cave. Part way through the night whenever the black lights came on I noticed a bright glow that seemed to be moving around the dance floor. I can remember thinking, "huh?" but never gave it much thought. Sometime during the night I happened to run into Bill and Greg when the black lights came on. That is when I found out the glow was Greg's feet. I mean Greg's shoes glowed so bright that it hurt your eyes to look directly at his feet. Greg had used monofilament fishing line to stitch his shoes with and it reacted very well with the black lights. If I remember correctly Greg went shoe shopping the following week.

Something Green

The single biggest day that occurred every year to our small town was the Fourth of July. On that day Peacham turned into a small city. By late morning of the fourth people started to show up on the ball field, which laid in a valley about in the middle of the village. Come early afternoon the parking spaces were getting scarce and at 1:00 the little league games started. If my memory serves me right there were three back to back ball games. Two bordering towns would send their teams and the winners of the first two games played a third. (As I was typing those last few words I began to realize how much, not only Peacham has lost over the years, but what all small towns have lost. When I grew up in that small Vermont town, us kids had everything. We had a little league team, a huge Fourth of July celebration complete with a fantastic fireworks show, a local Academy, which looked out over the ball field, and of course our very own ski tow. All of that is now gone and I am afraid never to return.)

When Kids Were Allowed to be Kids

Even forty plus years later I can still remember the excitement I felt when I was a young kid. There were people everywhere, all standing around in their own little groups. For some reason there always seemed to be a bunch of four or five young mothers standing near the concession stands each pushing a stroller. The group of big kids would move around slowly as they stood telling lies to one another and every once in a while they would toss out a firecracker, which back then was illegal to have. My group would stay just out of reach of the big kids, in hopes that they would break down, from our constant whining, and sell us some firecrackers at unheard of prices. Then every once in a while we would hear a swear word, which was a big deal. I remember one year when this group of big kids had moved close to the group of mothers with strollers. My mom happened to be in this group with my youngest brother Dean in the stroller. All of a sudden one of the big kids, David I think, threw a firecracker at one of the toughest kids Peacham had. Tom, out of instinct, jumped backwards and slammed right into Dean. Before Tom hit the ground mom had him by the scruff of the neck and picked him right off his feet. This was a hard blow to the image Tom had worked so hard to get.

All through the afternoon one of my friend's father was kept busy with his old fifteen gallon milk can. (Back in the early 60's many of the farmers still shipped their milk in these metal cans which had handle on each side and a metal lid that had to be driven on.) My friend's father, Frank, had an old milk can he had drilled a small hole in about an inch or so from the bottom. To this day I don't know what Frank poured into this can but after he had finished with the pouring he would drive the lid on, bend over and put a firecracker in the drilled hole, he would then light the firecracker and run for all he was worth. A few seconds later there would be this horrible explosion and if you were within about fifty feet of the can you could even feel the ground shake. The lid would take off and actually go right out of sight. As I remember, as soon as anyone heard the explosion all eyes were glued to the sky until the lid had landed, hopefully somewhere safe. One fourth the milk can finally gave its last performance. I remember watching Frank bend over to light the firecracker, take off running then we all heard the familiar explosion. This time though the lid stayed on and the bottom blew out. I swear the can went fifteen to twenty feet in the air. It came down bottom first and drove itself into the field. It was in so deep that it took Frank a few minutes to get it out.

    After the ball games were over the cars started to really roll in and filled the field to overflowing. There is a long gradual slope to the ball field below and cars would line up on this slope. A perfect spot to watch the fireworks. I am telling you, being a kid waiting for the night to get dark enough for the show to start, was all but unbearable. Time seemed to stop. Mom used to bring a blanket for us to sit on to watch the fireworks, as did many families. Dad was never able to join us, because like all the other fathers, he belonged to the Men's Club and had to work the concession stands and shoot off the fireworks.

One Fourth, when the fireworks were over, I realized I was on the blanket alone. I picked the blanket up and headed to the car. When I opened the door I saw Greg had his head in mom's lap and mom had the car flashlight, looking in Greg's ear. Now there is something you don't see any more, the car flashlight. For those of you that are not familiar with the cars from the late fifties and early sixties, all of those cars were made of metal, inside and out, including the dash. Almost every car had a flashlight with a magnet on the side of it, resting on top the dash. I asked mom what she was doing? Mom said, " Greg thinks there is something green in his ear". Greg swore up and down that he didn't put anything in his ear but he was sure there was something green in there.

About Wednesday of the following week Greg came clean. Earlier in the spring, Greg had been sitting at the end of our dooryard waiting for dad to pick him up so he could go on dad's egg route with him. Greg got bored and put three choke cherries in one ear and two came out. By the time mom got Greg to the doctor's the choke cherry had ripened and turned red. Greg did end up breaking his ear drum but like always Greg found a way to put that to good use. Whenever Greg gets sick of listening to anyone or there is a lot of noise when he wants to go to sleep, he just put his bad ear up.

A Ditch For All Seasons

Sandwiched between my parent's driveway and the field that belonged to the farm that Dave lived on was the ditch. This field had quite a slope to it as it stretched from the big light brown barn down to where it stopped abruptly and then there was about a three foot drop to our dooryard. At the base of the drop off was the ditch which ran the whole length of the driveway. At its narrowest point it was only a foot wide and in the widest part was close to three feet ,and this ditch gave us something to play in during all the seasons Vermont could throw at us.

During the winter months Dad would drive into the dooryard with his jeep and the plow would be angled so the snow was piled into this ditch. Over time the ditch would fill and then the snow was pushed up against the bank holding the field in place which made for even a bigger drop off to the driveway.

I remember one winter day when Greg and I were six and eight years old respectively and we stood in the garage looking up at the big brown barn and the field that ran down to our house and the big pile of snow that Dad and his jeep had piled up. Greg and I looked at one another and we had snow jump written all over our faces. We both grabbed a shovel and went to work hoping Mom didn't see what we were up to. The snow flew in every direction as Greg and I worked as fast as we could and after what seemed like a lifetime of work we were finished and as far as we knew we had gotten away with it because Mom hadn't yelled at us. I am telling you this jump was a work of art something both Greg and I were very proud of.

    The following day was Saturday, so just as soon as Greg and I finished gulping down breakfast we mentioned as casually as we could sound, that we thought we would go sliding instead of watching cartoons. Both of us hoping that we hadn't given away the snow jump. All Mom said was, "okay." Greg and I looked at one another, smiled and ran as fast as we could for the laundry room to put on our winter clothes, then just before we bolted out the door Mom yelled out, "Stay away from the jump at the end of the field."

    Two very sad little boys then walked out to the garage and dragged their sleds outside. After a few runs down the hill Greg and I figured Mom wouldn't be watching every minute and besides that what could go wrong if we happen to accidentally hit the jump. Not being able to decide which one of us should be the first to try out the jump we dug out the toboggan, that way be both could be first.

Mom later said that she was baking something in the kitchen when the laundry door burst open and these two kids, both blue in the face, came running in, dropped to the floor and flopped around while gasping for air. Shortly after the color returned to our face and the air to our lungs, Greg and I were once again able to talk and both of us stuck to the story that we accidentally hit the jump. Besides that there was no way to steer a toboggan anyways. After Greg and I drank the hot chocolate Mom made for us we went back outside and the last words we heard were again, "Stay away from the jump." As soon as we were out of hearing range of Mom, Greg and I started to wonder out loud what had gone wrong. After all the jump looked as impressive as any we had ever seen on TV. In the end both Greg and I figured that we must have done something wrong. Never once did we ever realize that all the people that jumped on TV landed on the steep part of the hill and not on a flat dooryard. Mom said about half to three quarters of an hour later the laundry door burst open, two kids came running in, dropped to the floor and started to flop around.

In the spring all the snow would melt and fill this ditch with water and all the life that came along with the warm temperatures, like frogs by the hundreds, poly wogs, lizards, salamanders and water spiders. Then in late spring the evening would be filled with the sound of the peepers as all the frogs called out with their songs of love. By the noise they made you would swear there was a thousand or more frogs in this ditch. Of course all a kid heard was come play in the water with us and that is exactly what we did. Day after day Dave would show up and we would see who could catch the most frogs, water spiders or lizards. One day all three of us, Dave, Greg and I were lined up catching frogs when this horrible scream shattered the sound of the crickets in the field above us. Dave and I instantly took off running as fast as we could around the end of the house towards the garden where Mom was working. As Dave and I rounded the porch, still side by side something blew by us at an incredible speed. Somehow Dave and I picked it up a notch but we weren't even able to close the distance on what was running in front of us, which turned out to be Greg.

 Moments later we were all huddled around Mom. Finally between gasps for air Greg was able to tell us that he was going for a frog and came up with a snake, which evidently was going for the same frog. We never did find out what happened to the frog.

 A few years later a couple of our friends were spending the afternoon at our house. That made four of us, two more than the minimum number needed for a ball game. Sometime during the game Albert hit the ball and Harold went running for it. As fast as Harold's legs could carry him he came back with the ball and tried to tag Albert out. Somehow they got their feet tangled up and both went down, Harold first. When the dust cleared Harold was yelling at Albert to get off. Harold's feet were on one side of the ditch and his hands on the other side and it looked like he was doing a push up with the old dirty ditch water beneath him and Albert on top of him. I got to laughing so hard that I never did see what happen but neither Harold or Albert got wet.

I also remember one early spring day when neither Greg or I could wait to start playing baseball. It was quite chilly out and still patches of snow on the ground where the sun didn't hit. We decided that Greg would pitch first so I was at home plate holding the bat ready to knock the ball out of the dooryard. It was cold enough out that I had on a pair of deerskin gloves which, unknown to me had become wet and slippery. Greg pitched the ball and with all my might I swung at it and the bat came flying out of my hands, right at Greg. I stood there and watched the bat, which looked like a boomerang, go right for Greg. Greg saw it too and jumped as high as he could and screamed. This bat pulled Greg out of the air and dropped him to the ground like a lead weight. Oh man was he ever mad.

Years later, when we were in high school and I had my driver's license, a bunch of us kids were standing around, my parent's car on the first day of fishing season. Even though there were still patches of snow around especially in the woods next to the brooks, it was the first day of fishing and we were trying to decide where we should go. Off in the far distance we heard a very faint humming noise that seemed to be getting closer and louder. The humming noise was soon replaced by the familiar buzzing of a bee. Moments later Albert yelled and again the buzzing faded to a hum until it disappeared all together.

Summer, "63"

The summer months of my youth hold many and special memories, too many, I am sure, to recall them all. Many of those early summer days found me fishing with either my brother, Greg, or with friends that lived in our small town of Peacham. The summer of 63 has gone down in my personal history as the summer of water walking and fishing. That summer found Larry, a kid that lived about a half a mile away, and myself with a common desire. The desire to catch every fish that lived in the brook that flowed in the valley between our two houses. That desire to fish lived for many years inside of myself and brought me in contact with many reptiles, mostly snakes, although one time it was lizards.

On the lizard occasion, I was night fishing with my neighbor Dave. We had a big bonfire going and sitting by the fishing access of a nearby pond, watching our lines that were in the water. All of a sudden, in the flickering light of the fire, something caught my eye. I asked Dave to turn the flashlight on and walking between Dave and me and on both sides of us were dozens of lizards. And these were big lizards, each were a half a foot long or more. That only happened once and to this day I don't know why we were caught in that stampede of lizards. Maybe it was spawning season or something.

I remember one summer day when my brother Greg, myself and our friend Jeff, got up very early and started the three and a half to four mile walk, in the dark, to a beaver dam. This beaver dam we caught sight of the fall before when we were riding with my dad. We would have never seen this dam if the leaves were still on the trees but as luck would have it one of us happened to catch a glimpse of the water as we drove slowly along looking for partridge. The wait for winter to get over and for fishing season to start just about killed us. But the thought of pulling monster native trout out of this hidden beaver dam kept us going.

Fishing season did finally arrive but there was way too much snow in the woods to even think about fishing this beaver dam so the wait continued. Then one morning we woke up and the moment we walked outside and took one deep breath of air we knew summer had arrived. That Sunday morning as Greg, Jeff and I stumbled along the dirt road in the dark, sometimes walking off the road and falling into the ditch, we kept our dream of catching huge hungry fish alive by our constant talking. Before we even got to the beaver dam we had convinced ourselves that on our way back we would have to stop at one of the houses that we walked by and ask if we could use their phone to call one of our parents to come and get us. We would then have to explain that the fish we caught weighed so much that we couldn't carry them any farther. Then as we walked outside to wait for our parents to show up, we decided that it was only right if we left these nice people with a couple of our huge native trout.

Just as the sky was starting to get light we were standing on the steep bank that led down to the beaver dam. The light was still very dim and after many falls we found ourselves standing by the edge of the water. We were so excited that our fingers couldn't work fast enough to get the worm on our hooks. Finally the sun started to beat down on the bank and on us with its unrelenting heat. With the sun came light and we could see why the trip down the bank was so hard and why each of us were bleeding in several places. The bank was covered with loose gravel and rocks ranging from about a foot in diameter to two and a half feet, many with sharp edges. We were also able to take a closer look at the beaver dam only to discover that we had been fishing in about a six inches of water which was lined with tree branches and by then most of our fish hooks. We fished for about another hour before the dam took our last hook and never once gave us a single bite. Exhausted from the heat and disappointment we turned around to try to climb out. That was when we discovered that the bank seemed to be moving. As it turned out it was moving. Jeff didn't even have to take a step, he just bent down and picked up three snakes and threw them into the water to watch them swim. I don't have any idea how many snakes were on this bank but it was alive with them. I am not sure what Greg or Jeff did but I took a couple of deep breaths, closed my eyes and took off on a dead run, hoping I knew enough to stop running when I hit the dirt road.

Years later, when I was a teenager and a few of my friends had cars, we once again got into fishing. This one Sunday morning Albert, Burt and I took off for, "The Dam"., "The Dam" sat on the Connecticut River and just below the dam rumor had it that the fish were really biting. To get to a really big pool of water we had to walk down a path that had been chiseled out of ledge. I was walking right behind Albert when he vanished. I never saw or heard him move. One minute I was looking at the back of Albert and the next moment he wasn't any where in sight. About that time I looked to my left and that was when Burt discovered that both Albert and I had vanished. Sitting right at eye level on a big flat rock was this huge green snake all curled up with its tongue darting in and out. Much to both Albert's and my horror Burt tried to catch the snake. Thank God it got away from him.

Well, back to the summer of 63'. One night, after dinner, I rushed over to Larry's and we started fishing right behind his house. The land leveled out and there was a long 150 foot or so stretch of slow moving deep water. At the end of this stretch of slow moving water was an old tree that had, years before, fallen. This tree acted just like a dam and there was a very deep pool of water on the upper side and below the tree was another large deep pool. The water had rushed over the tree, much like a waterfall and dug its own pool. Larry was fishing on the upper side and I grabbed a spot on the lower side.

When Larry and I first headed out with our poles we met his older brother, Bobby. Bobby had a hammer and a crow bar in his hands. He was going to tear down an old shed that was no longer being used. After Larry and I had been fishing for about twenty minutes the hairs on the back of my neck started to stand up. Even though I hadn't heard a sound over the roar of the water as it flowed over the tree and into the pool down below something inside of me told me to turn around. All I saw, about a foot from my face, was a half a dozen or so snakes and their heads wrapping around themselves. About two or maybe three hundredths of a second later I was standing on the other side of the brook, with my fishing pole still in my hand, looking at Bobby holding a whole handful of snakes. Bobby had found a nest of snakes in the shed and mistakenly thought we might like to see them.

After a few minutes I once again started to breathe and that is when I noticed that my feet were still dry. Later Larry told me that when I took off running I looked like one of those lizards in the dessert that run on their hind feet across the hot sand.

Camp

Sometime during the early 1960's Greg and I started to hear our parents talk about a camp, something that grabbed our attention. I had seen part of a fairly new movie, "The Parent Trap" and the part that I saw looked like everyone was having a lot of fun, although I didn't know how it turned out. I am sure some of you have never heard of this movie., "The Parent Trap" came out in 1961 and it is about identical twin sisters that were separated at birth. Years later, when the girls were young teenagers, they ran into one another at a girls camp and from what I had seen of this movie, camps were a great place to be.

A few years earlier my parents had bought an older home just outside of Peacham village. This home had originally been heated by an old hot air furnace, so in all of the upstairs rooms there were hot air registers with small louvers. These louvers could be opened at will so during the winter months hot air had a way of getting to the upper floors. The register in my bedroom was right above the fancy dining room and right off the fancy dining room was the living room. I accidentally found out if a movie came on that my parents didn't want me to watch, usually because it came on too late, I could very silently lift the register up and stick my head through the floor and by cocking it at an unnatural angle I could watch TV. Many nights I would get such a bad headache after 15 or 20 minutes that I would have to quit, put the register back and go to bed, but on other nights I could make the whole movie. Mom made a habit of checking on us boys when she went to bed and on several occasions she would find me fast asleep on the floor with my head stuck down through the ceiling.

One Sunday afternoon, in between chores that is, dad said, "come on boys your mom and I want to show you the camp we bought." Greg and I took off running and had a fight to see who could get in the car first, why we always did this I do not know. Less than fifteen minutes later we all stood in the woods looking at the water. I couldn't hide my disappointment; it didn't look anything like the camp did in the movie. What mom and dad bought was a piece of wooded land next to the water.

Even though both Greg and I were quite young, we were expected to help with the clearing of the land. Dad wouldn't let either Greg or I near an ax so our job turned out to be lugging brush to a growing pile and to pile the wood as dad cut it. I kinda pity dad because looking back, I don't ever remember seeing a chain saw at camp, in fact the first chain saw

I ever saw was the one I bought so I could use the engine to go on a go cart I was building, another story for another time. I do remember seeing an old buck saw so I can only assume dad had to cut every tree with that old hand saw.

Greg and I had to do a lot of waiting around for dad to cut the trees up, so to fill this free time Greg and I would fight, the way most brothers do at that age. About the time we got on dad's nerves he would decide that we had piled the wood in the wrong place so we would have to lug it all to another spot. On a particularly bad Sunday Greg and I would have to move that wood pile four or five times. I can remember how disgusted and mad Greg and I would get at dad for not being able to make up his mind where he wanted the wood pile, never once did we connect the dots.

By the fall of the first year deep holes had been dug, squared off old railroad ties leveled and the floor joists were laid on top of them. Floor joists are two by eight inch planks that are stood up edgeways and the building is built on top of them. As a kid these joists were fun to run across, that is until you slipped on one of them and straddled it on the way down. I can still remember hearing a blood curdling scream and then seeing Greg's motionless body sprawled across the unfinished floor.

The following spring, it became apparent to dad, that a lot of fill was going to have to be hauled into camp to make the land level. Somewhere dad found an old dump truck some farmer had, years earlier, retired. I can remember the comments dad made about how cheap the farmer sold him the dump truck. It wasn't long before dad found out there was reason it was so cheap; this truck had a few nasty habits and as it turned out dad also had a few bad habits.

    Greg and I used to love to go with dad when he hauled fill or gravel to farmers or to camp, with the truck. We usually got to hear a bunch of swear words and it wasn't uncommon for us to see dad in an awkward spot before the night was over. I can't begin to tell you how many times dad would forget to release the tailgate when he put the body up to dump the gravel. In my mind I can still hear the old truck whine as dad raced the engine to make the dump body go up and just when you thought everything had come to a stop the cab of the truck would shoot about ten feet in the air. Dad would look out the driver's window with a sheepish grin on his face and wonder how he would get out of that one. Sometimes dad would have to crawl out of the truck, especially if there wasn't an adult there to shovel the dirt out of the back of the truck, and shovel it himself. Time and time again after dad and the truck were both back on the ground he would forget to release the PTO lever and head down the road all the time the body would be lifting up and sometimes Greg and I were in the back.

    The truck also liked to quit running all on its own and you never knew when that might happen, sometimes it was when you were going around a sharp corner and other times it was when you were going down a very steep hill. Another thing it liked to do was to shake. I have seen times when dad would hit a bump just right and the steering wheel would start to shake. Soon the whole truck would shake so bad that dad's hat would be bouncing on his head and it was all he could do to hang onto the steering wheel. The only way dad could get this shaking to quit was to come to a complete stop and after a minute or so we would be back on our way……..

I am afraid I will have to get back to this story at a later date, I am out of time. Until then…

The Ski Tow

During the summer months the Peacham Ski Tow was part of an active farm located on the main road between Peacham and Danville. This hill that the ski tow was on was very steep and about a third of the way down had one very large knoll surrounded by several smaller ones. These knolls were good for the daring skier that wanted to use them for a jump. That is unless there was another skier that happened to be on the landing site, which happened more often than one might think. On a flat area at the foot of this steep hill were two shacks. One housed the old ford flat head V8 engine that ran the rope tow and the second building housed a small snack bar, complete with a popcorn popper, a grill for frying dogs & burgers and

in one corner was an old stove that once in a while even put out heat. The entire front of the ski shack was windows so those that came in to grab a bite to eat and get warmed up could watch the skiers as they shot down the hill.

As steep and dangerous as this hill was there were not that many serious injuries. Oh sure we had our share of broken legs, arms, collar bones and one poor soul even got his jacket wound up in the tow rope and went through the pulleys at the top of the hill, but aside from that not much happened.

During the late 60's the place to be on Saturday and Sunday afternoon was The Ski Tow. High school kids were using anything they could find to ski on. One kid by the name of Chris found an old pair of military skis hiding in the garage above the family car. Probably put there by Chris's dad in hopes that he wouldn't find them. Well Chris was a fairly short person and the skis were at least seven feet in length, they also had the old military boot bindings that you couldn't get out of even if you wanted to. I mean you could slam into a tree and your skis broken into tiny pieces and yet your boot would still be shackled to what was left. Even with this combination Chris mastered the skis and the hill and became one of the faster skiers. One Sunday afternoon I was just above the big knoll when Chris went flying by, hit one of the smaller knolls and took to the air. He was wearing a tuque which had a three and a half to four foot tassel on it and he looked kinda cool when he shot by with this tassel snapping in the wind behind him. Moments later I heard this yelling which sounded a lot like, "Help Me", "Help Me" I then heard the familiar voice of Bobby, another excellent skier, yell out, "quick Chris is hanging upside down". My eyes then looked towards the yelling and sticking just above the smaller knoll I could see the backs of Chris skis, sticking straight in the air, and they were crossed at the top. I took off skiing towards Chris and when I rounded the knoll I could see that soon after Chris shot over the knoll he went head first and drove the tips of his skis in the snow. His ski poles were driven into the snow in front of him and he was holding himself up with them, his tassel was swinging back and forth just brushing the snow. Before I could get to Chris, Bobby had picked him up and gotten the tip of the skis out of the snow.

    A few years later I found myself taking care of the shack. My job included selling tickets, making coffee, hot chocolate, popcorn, dogs & burgers. I really liked this job because it gave me the chance to make a little spending money and watch other people wipe out on skis instead of me being one of them. One afternoon I happened to look out just in time to see some little kid going way too fast as he sliced down the hill. Moments later I could see this kid's skis start to hop up and down and then all I could see was a big cloud of snow. After the snow settled this kid picked himself up, grabbed his skis and started walking towards the shack, dragging his skis behind him. It wasn't long before I could see that it was my youngest brother Dean, he was kinda whimpering with a few tears coming down his face. About that time I happened to notice that he was walking in his stocking feet and his ski boots were still on his skis. When he finally reached the shack I hollered out and told him to quit crying. I said, "Nobody likes a whiner" and, "put your boots back on before you catch a cold. So that is what Dean did and went back to skiing.

    Once in a while a skier would underestimate their speed and the distance to the shack and slam into it. The inside of the shack was all open and it was really loud and would echo and shake when a skier hit the shack. We would always run outside to look at the unlucky person laying on the ground. Everyone of them looked like a fish out of water, with their mouth opening and closing as they tried to get oxygen back into their lungs. My memory tells me that we never offered to help, we just looked.

A New Word

The first thing I learned on my first day as a first grader came about half way through the morning. So far that day things had not gone all that well and I was not the only kid that felt that way. Earlier the summer before that first day of school, my mom had taken me to a farm  in East Peacham so I could meet a kid by the name of Bill. Up until then my whole life had revolved around the poultry farm and our next door neighbor Dave and of course my brother Greg, who was two years younger than I was . Dave was five years older than I was, so as far as I knew I was the only kid my age. Bill and I were about a month apart in age and instantly became friends and spent the afternoon playing cops and robbers, a popular game back then.

Peacham was a very small town that had three school houses for the grades one through six, with two grades in each classroom. I can still remember the fear I felt when I saw all the other kids for the first time. I think mom knew I would be in for a shock and that is why we visited Bill, at least that way I would know one kid. About mid morning the teacher, a rather beefish stout woman, said, "Alright, time for recess." "Oh man", I thought to myself, "what now." So far that morning two of the new kids had cried and one got so scared that she left a puddle on the floor by her seat. About then one of the big kids, a second grader, smacked me behind the head and said, "Come on idiot, it is time to go outside and play." For a brief moment I thought I might have had this school thing all wrong but then recess was over and we had to return to our seat, that is if you could remember which seat was yours.

Recess, as it turned out, was where the first graders did most of their learning, early on that is. And one of the first things you learned was not to do what the big kids told you to do, even if you were threatened. We later found out that we were learning something called common sense. That lesson was driven home on the swing set the first day we had a hard frost. The first and second grade school had a fantastic handmade swing set. The swing part was constructed out of old telephone poles with three swings hanging by old rusty chains and off to one side was a huge store bought slide. On the first really cold day of fall, the slide was all white with frost when we first arrived at school. By the time recess came around it was warming up but still cold enough outside that you could see your breath when you breathed out. As soon as we were outside and out of sight of the teacher the big kids told us that the slide tasted like chocolate and we should stick our tongues on it. Moments later the teacher came out with her kettle of warm water and poured it down the slide. Later that morning Bill said, "I can't wait until next year when we can teach the little kids some common sense."

Most of the time the boys and girls played separately with the boys playing cops and robbers and I guess the girls must have played with dolls or something. Cops and robbers was a lot of fun but there was one big kid, Larry, that we were sure cheated. The unwritten rule was if you were shot you were supposed to drop dead and stay that way until the game was over. Time and time again one of us little kids would draw a bead on Larry with our stick and yell out BANG. Larry would drop to the ground and do a fantastic acting job of dying, just like in the real westerns. We would blow away the imaginary smoke from our stick and put it in back in our holster, just in time to see Larry jump up grab his arm and run around the corner. All of this happened so fast that you didn't have time to get your stick out of the holster to shoot him again so you would run after him. Then the second you ran around the corner

Larry would shoot you and you couldn't argue with him because he was a big kid.

I think the second new word I learned was, "Clean Your Clock." It was a girl by the name of Evelyn that taught all of us boys in first grade that one. Then when she was convinced that we wouldn't forget she proceeded to teach the second grade boys. Evelyn came from a family of mostly big brothers and she knew moves that none of us had even heard of. Evelyn became very popular when it came time for picking teams for the ball game of keep away, one of the few games that we all played together. Evelyn was always the first one chosen and her team always won. Later on in life, like in the fifth and sixth grade, us boys would talk among ourselves. One of us might say well I am all done taking crap from Evelyn and the next time the opportunity arises I am going to show her once and for all. Thank god that opportunity never arose. I can just imagine how embarrassing it would be to get your Clock Cleaned by a girl when you were in the sixth grade.

The long noon recess at the third and fourth grade school brought something new called story time. Our teacher thought up the story time idea after what came to be known as the Merle Incident happened. After the bell rang to signal the end of recess the desks were filled with boys that were covered with sweat and wired tight. So wound up that they had not calmed down enough to even sit still, let alone learn anything. One day the teacher was walking between two rows of desk, soon after the noon recess, when she stopped and bent over to pick up a piece of paper that laid on the floor. Merle took that opportunity to stand behind this large wide teacher and pretend that he was going to kick her in the back side. Much to Merle's horror and our humor his shoe came off and nailed the teacher dead center. As big as this teacher was she was very fast and before Merle could even get the hideous scared look to leave his face, Mrs. Watson had him by the ear. Together they headed towards the dreaded back room, with Mrs. Watson dragging Merle and Merle limping. A few minutes later the back room door opened Merle slowly walked back to his desk and put his shoe back on, which some kid had kindly put on top of his desk.

The next day Mrs. Watson announced that she was going to read to us each day after the noon recess, so we could have the time to calm down a bit. I remember one story about a kid by the name of Theodore and this kid had everything like a pony with a cart and all kinds of toys to play with. Well this happened the fall after the summer that my family spent at the newly opened race track in Waterford. Every Saturday night my dad and his best friend Frank Foss would take my brother Greg, myself and the two older Foss girls, Sharon and Maxine, to the races. It wasn't long before I just knew that when I grew up I had to be a race car driver. My favorite race car driver was Glenn Andrews and Greg's favorite driver was Ronnie Marvin. So when Greg and

I were not at the races rooting for our favorite driver we were kept busy fighting over which one was the best driver. That was also the summer my mom was pregnant with what turned out to be my youngest brother Dean. I was bound and determined that if it was a boy we were going to name him Theodore Andrew and there was no talking me out of it. Finally dad asked me if I knew how to spell Theodore and I had to admit I didn't., "Well" dad said, " if you can't spell it how do you expect a baby to spell it." He had me on that one.

That was also the fall that us boys really got into playing football. According to the teacher we were supposed to play something called touch football. We played behind the school, in a small field that the teacher couldn't see from inside the classroom, so touch football soon became tackle football and everyone was happy. Every day, when the recess was over, we would bring the football inside and we kept it under the chair that Mrs. Watson sat in to read to us. One day the football blew up and in that one room school house it sounded like a shot gun blast going off. When Mrs. Watson was on her way back down to the chair, soon after the screaming stopped, we learned yet another new word, a swear one this time.

School Bus Blues

The other morning, when Dave showed up for work, early as usual, he was carrying the morning newspaper, also usual. On the front page was an article about the latest campus shooting, where a student shot a security guard and them himself. This story got both Dave and myself to reminiscing about our days in school and how much they have changed. Dave is five years older than I am and as we talked we began to realize that things had started to change when we were kids. They were slow in coming and neither one of us saw them as changes…..but change they did.

Our early morning conversation seemed to get stuck on the school buses that we used to ride and the things that, back then, were common and no one thought much about until we took the time to look back. Before I type another word I first must , once again, remind all of you that our small town of Peacham is a very rural setting, more so back in the 60's than now. Back in the 50 and 60's Peacham was a big farming community with hunting and fishing being a big part of life. Almost everyone owned a gun and hunting was not only popular but in many cases a necessity to put food on the table. Fishing was also a way of keeping our dinner plates full. …. Which reminds me of a visitor we had at our church. Somehow our minister had arranged for a missionary from Korea to join our little community for a week. This visitor, I have long forgotten his name, spent most of the week visiting different families, joining them for the evening meal and talking about his time in Korea during the war. Our family was one of the families that he visited, mom however was at a loss as to what to serve for supper. Mom then remembered that we had a freezer full of brook trout, thanks to Greg and me and figured how could she go wrong serving fish to someone from an Asian country. That night, at the dinner table, this visitor watched as we all pulled the fins out of the fish and scraped the meat off all the bones and then ate the meat. This man from Korea followed our led by cutting the tail off the fish and piled them in one corner with all the fins and bones. He then ate the meat and when he was finished he ate the fins, tails and bones. Mom talked about this for years.

    The first school bus I rode on was, I am sure, an old panel truck that had been converted to a bus. It was green in color and the passenger front seat had been removed so the kids could have easy access, that is the young kids, the big kids, had to walk almost doubled over. We then sat on bench type seats that had been bolted down to the floor and we sat looking at one another. Whenever the bus driver had to make a sudden stop all of us kids ended up in a big pile at the front of the bus.

By the time I entered third grade we were riding in a factory bought yellow school bus. This new bus also brought a new driver and the new driver was a farmer that had more than a dozen kids. Riding the bus, back then was a big and fun part of having to go to school. This bus driver was a lenient man and allowed us to sit where and with who we wanted to. He also allowed us to make noise as long as it didn't get out of hand. At about that age all of the boys couldn't wait to drive and many of the older kids had already built their own doddle bugs, as they were called. These doddle bugs were old cars or pickups that had been shortened, the rear wheel brought up right behind the rear of the front seat and, of course, all the doors removed. That is unless you were David. (More about Dave's doddle bug in another story) One of the boy's favorite pastimes, was to watch the bus driver so he could learn how to drive a vehicle with a standard transmission. Finally one day one of the older kids, Peter I think it was, sat in the back of the bus and held his book like a steering wheel. He would then make noises like the bus and would double shift when the bus driver did and even make the screeching noise as the bus came to a stop. The following day there were eight to ten of us boys sitting in the back of the bus holding books.

Something else that could be found on the school bus, during deer season that is, was the bus driver's hunting rifle. It laid on the floor on the left side of the driver's seat. During the two weeks of deer season all of us kids were quiet, not out of fear of the gun but we were all busy looking for deer. If we got lucky enough to see a deer and the driver shot it, it would mean we would be late for school.

By the time I entered third grade Dave was already in junior high which was housed in the building that was home to Peacham Academy, a short walking distance from Dave's house. Dave never rode the bus when the driver carried his gun but Dave remembered getting on the school bus when he was in fifth and sixth grade carrying a shot gun. When the bus arrived at school the teacher would take all of the shot guns and stand them up in one corner. Then at the end of the day when school was over the boys would grab their guns, walk outside and load them while they were still on school property. That was about the time the bragging started as each kid relived some fantastic shot that he was sure only a person with his skills, could have made. Thank God they never got that mad at one another, after all they did have loaded guns in their hands.... I never knew the boys were allowed to bring guns to school until Dave shared this story with me. I guess that is one of the changes we never saw coming.

Doodle Bugs I Have Known

Over the years I have been associated with several doodle bugs and have actually had the privilege of owning one and two pre-doodle bugs. The first time I ever heard about a doodle bug was from my neighbor and mentor Dave. Dave was our closest neighbor, he was five years older than I was, and he was always doing or building something really neat.

One day while Greg and I were walking home from the poultry farm, we noticed Dave had an old pickup in his dooryard that he was working on. It didn't take Greg or me very long to be standing by the pickup pestering Dave with a bunch of questions. , "What ya got there?" I asked, and Dave said a, "doodle bug" , "Huh" I said, "it looks a lot like an old rusted out beat up pickup to me." , "That" Dave said, "is because you are an idiot, now leave me alone." , "C'mon Dave" I blurted out, "I want to help., "No, you'll just get in the way, like you always do." , "No. I won't, Pleeeese", "Well okay, but you must promise you will do everything I say." Only later did it come to my attention that was a promise I should not have made.

Dave's doodle bug started life as a 1938 Ford pickup and by the time Dave got it, its life was almost over. The fenders were falling off, the doors no longer stayed closed and there were big holes in the bed of the truck and down through the floor of the cab. And the engine smoked so bad that after a minute of running you could no longer see the truck.

The first thing I helped Dave with was to strip the body of all unnecessary metal. This took a couple of days and when we were done all that was left of the original truck was the firewall, which still had the gauges, the brake, clutch and gas pedals, the emergency brake, shifting lever and the four wheels. Dave wanted to shorten the wheel base but wasn't sure what he should do with the gas tank so we removed the front seat, which was falling down through the floor any ways, and laid the gas tank sideways right behind the firewall. We then placed a blanket on it for cushion and called it a seat.

Somewhere Dave got his hands on a 1950 ford flat head V8 which he rebuilt in shop class at Peacham Academy. With help from some big kids from the Academy, Dave got the rebuilt engine in his soon to be running doodle bug. Luckily for Dave, I happened to show up, the day he tried to get the engine running. Dave had been working on it for a while but he didn't seem to be having much luck, it sure sounded like it wanted to run but just wouldn't go.

Finally Dave said, "I don't think it is getting any spark." (A phrase I would use countless times after that) I said, "What do you mean not getting spark?" , "Well" Dave, grumbled, , "you need to have an electrical spark come out of the coil, go into the distributor cap and from there the rotor will send it to the cylinder that is on compression." I said, "Oh yea", like I knew what he was talking about. Dave then said, "We better figure out where the problem is.", "Yea, I blurted out, "And just how are we going to do that?" Dave pulled the coil wire out of the distributor and said, "Here hold onto this wire and I'll show you." Dave then reached over the firewall and pushed on the starter button. I got up off the ground, brushed myself off and said, "Wow does that ever hurt.", "Well, Dave said, "we now know there is a really good spark coming out of the coil."

    Next Dave climbed off the engine and crossed his arms as he stood there thinking for a moment. That is when I heard a little ouch and Dave reached into his shirt pocket and pulled out the ignition rotor, which he had put there when he adjusted the points., "There", Dave said, "is another important lesson for you, always put small parts in your pocket when you work on cars or you might knock them off the engine and loose them.", "Now give me that screw driver so I can take the distributor cap off and put the rotor back in place." Dave then sat behind the steering wheel, hit the starter button again and the engine fired to life.

After a few more adjustments, we hopped onto the gas tank and headed for the back field, a field that had been mowed a few weeks earlier. This field was out of sight of the farm and one that his dad, Claude, probably wouldn't look at for a while, hopefully after our tire marks had disappeared. This back field was mostly a steep hill with a level flat spot at the base of it and at the end of this flat spot was a large stone wall that had stood for a hundred years or more. This doodle bug ran like a top and shot up the hill with very little effort and I swear we even gained speed as we went up. Once at the top Dave took about six turns on the steering wheel before the doodle bug even began to change direction. "Remind me to look at that when we get back", Dave hollered at me. Whenever you were near the doodle bug and it was running you had to yell, there was no exhaust on it. , "OK", I yelled back.

Once we got turned around Dave tromped onto the gas to see just how much power it had and to see how far he could make the rear wheels spin. About a third of the way down the hill the doodle bug caught up with the wheels and Dave figured it was time to start slowing down. That was about the time we found out that six inch high grass, when wet with dew, is almost as slippery as ice. Especially when the tread on the tire was something that used to be there years before. It didn't take long to get to the flat spot at the foot of the hill and the stone wall was coming up fast. The loud screaming was hurting my ears so I covered my left ear with my left hand and my eyes with the other hand and closed my mouth as tight as I could, I sure didn't want to get picked on by Dave for screaming like a baby, but the screaming continued to ring in my ears. I then worked up enough nerve to peak out through my fingers that covered my eyes. Dave's mouth was wide open, the whites of his eyes were showing and his face was all twisted and looked hideous. He was pushing on the brake pedal with both feet and his hands were just a blurr as he cranked on the steering wheel, trying to keep the doodle bug going somewhat straight. Once again I closed my eyes and this time I took up religion. A few moments later the wind against my face stopped and all I could feel was a violent shaking. Cautiously I opened my eyes, Dave knuckles were as white as his face and both feet were still trying to push the brake pedal through the floor board.

….After a few more seconds I was able to force my heart out of my throat and back down into my chest and I yelled at Dave, "Oh Man, I got to get me one of these."

The Old, "38" Dodge Pickup

By the time Dave and I had lugged all of the scattered rocks back to the stone wall; it was time for me to rush home for dinner. I had suggested that we leave the hole, put a board across and call it a gate but like all disputes, that is all the time, Dave was bigger than I was. We settled them Dave's way and that way was to wrestle for the answer.

As soon as the doodle bug screeched to a halt in front of Dave's big old barn, I was off running towards home. I burst through the front door covered with sweat and dirt and I was wired tight. As fast as I could I washed off the dirt or, I should say, the dirt you could see, and I slid into my seat at the dinner table. The dinner table, back then, was a place for each of us to share our day with one another. Looking back I can safely say it was a special time for everyone. Dad worked on the poultry farm and came home every night at 5pm to a hot meal that mom had just put on the table. I can remember a time when I was about six years old and my brother Greg was four. Dad's nightly ritual, after work that is, was to wash his face, shave then rinse the rest of the shaving cream off. For some reason the shaving fascinated both Greg and myself so, after dad was done shaving, Greg and I would take turns lathering up with hand soap and then take one of dad's old razors, the one without the blade in it, and shave the soap off our faces. One night when I was finished shaving, Greg took his turn and a few minutes later came walking into the dining room and blood was coming out of a good half dozen places on his face. Mom grabbed Greg and back to the bathroom they went. The next time I saw Greg his face was covered with tiny pieces of toilet paper. The dinner table was a very enjoyable part of our day.

    The moment there was a break in the nightly conversation I let loose, telling about my day and Dave's doodle bug. I figured it was best if I left the ride down the steep hill out of my story and to this day I still think it was the right decision. I was soon bugging dad about him helping me find an old pickup I could make a doodle bug out of. At the time I was flat busted broke so I reminded dad that the price would have to be pretty cheap. Much to my surprise and delight dad knew of such a pickup. As it turned out it was the truck that sat right behind our very own barn, a pickup I had completely forgotten about.

    This was Grandpa Dick's old pickup. Grandpa Dick, my mother's dad, had bought a newer truck and thought my dad might be able to put his old pickup to use on the farm, so he drove it to our place and just left it. There was, however, one catch. The pickup needed a battery and if I wanted to use the truck I had to buy the battery with my own money. We were just heading into fall, so every penny I earned while working on the poultry farm went into a special hiding place and, come spring, I had saved enough for the battery.

    I hate to admit this but it took me quite a while to find where the battery went. Believe it or not the floor was made out of wood and you had to very carefully lift one corner of the floor and thread it up over the shifting and emergency brake levers. Under this floor was a tray for the battery and attached to the underside of the brake pedal was the master cylinder. The battery, once filled with water, was a lot heavier than I had planned on, but after a bit I got it in place and out of sheer luck hooked the cables to the right battery posts. I then smiled and reached for the ignition key only to find it missing. I immediately thought of Greg and hunted him down. After much interrogation, I came to the conclusion that he didn't know a thing about the key either.

    I ended up tearing the house, barn, pickup and even the old chicken coop apart but never did find the key. After another couple more weeks of working, I had enough money to buy an ignition key and switch. Wiring in an ignition switch turned out to be more challenging that I had expected and I finally had to ask dad for help. After dinner I dragged dad out behind the barn. This was even before he had the chance to read the paper. I stood there and watched him switch two wires and that was all it took. As soon as he turned the key to the on position the little green light on the dash lit up and dad stepped on the starter button which was on the floor by the gas pedal. The starter slammed into the flywheel and locked solid. Again the smile left my face.

I immediately started in on the long job of pulling the starter out. There was one bolt on top that was easy to see and get at. By twisting into an unnatural position I was able to feel two bolts underneath that had to come out. The top bolt was out in minutes and then I started in on the long process of taking one of the bottom bolts out. I worked until dark and still had a ways to go on the first unseen bolt. The next day, as soon as the morning chores and breakfast were over, I was back twisting myself into a deformed shape and went back to work on the starter bolt. A short while before I had to return to the farm to do the mid morning egg picking, I got the first lower bolt out. I tried then to wiggle the starter to see if it was a little loose but it was held tight in place by the third bolt.

Just before darkness consumed the day, I was able to get the third bolt out and as soon as I removed the starter I heard the starter gear slam back into place. I then turned the starter over to look at it. I noticed that it only had two mounting ears on it. I had spent hours pulling out a bolt that helped hold the transmission to the engine. At least with the starter out of the way the transmission bolt went back in place easily.

During the noon hour of day three, I dragged dad out behind the barn again and much to both of our surprise the old pickup started. I can still remember hearing it pop and bang as it came to life and after a few minutes it began to smooth out. The next thing I knew I saw dad put it in gear and the rear wheels began to throw dirt and slowly it began to move and moments later we were in front of the barn instead of behind it.

I couldn't wait to show Dave my new treasure but dad made it pretty clear I was not going to drive it up the road to Dave's place so I had to wait for Dave to find the time to stop in. Dave was just enough older than I was that he found girls interesting so I was in for a bit of a wait. One day Dave did stop in and he couldn't believe what good shape the old pickup was in and instantly tried to find a way to get the truck for his collection. I wouldn't budge so Dave convinced me that I should rebuild the pickup. After all, he said, "It only has a few tiny rust holes in the running boards and all the fenders were on it and solid."

This sounded like a really good idea to me so the next day, after dad took off for work; I drove the pickup into the garage and started to take it apart. It happened to be one of dad's long egg route days and by the time he got home for dinner I had the garage full of pickup parts. At dinner that night we talked mostly about my plans for the pickup. I told dad that I was going to rebuild it and that I hoped he didn't mind if I took over his garage while I did it. I said, "I don't think it will hurt your car at all to sit outside while I work on my truck." Dad then took a turn at expressing his thoughts and as it turned out my plans changed. The next morning I was to start putting the pickup back together.

When dad got home the next day, which was also a long egg route day, not only was the garage full of parts but also the small lawn in front of the garage. I figured the truck would go back together a lot quicker than coming apart and I would have the time to take it apart a little bit more. As it turned out I was much better at taking things apart than putting them back together. Not only could I not remember what part went where, but several of the parts I couldn't even remember taking off.

It took dad until the middle of the following week before he was able to get my pickup back together enough so it would move on its own. Years later dad made the mistake of asking me if I could find out why his pickup wouldn't run. I was sleeping in late that morning because I had taken a few days off from work before I had to take off for college. When dad was heading out of the dooryard, that morning, his pickup quit running. One of my friends, Burt, had just finished working with a local plumber so I called him and asked if he wanted to help. Well neither Burt nor I had any clue as to what we were doing, so we just started to take parts off and look at them. If we didn't see anything wrong we put them in the cab of the truck and take off another part. After the cab was full we started to fill the pickup bed. By the end of the day we had parts everywhere and still no idea why the truck wouldn't run. As it turned out that was okay because the next day was Saturday and no parts stores were open, so we couldn't have fixed the pickup anyways. The next day was Sunday and that afternoon I took off for college and Burt left to live with his grandmother in a town forty miles away. When I drove out of the dooryard the last thing I saw in my rear view mirror was dad. He was just standing there, with his hands in his pants pocket, looking at his pickup.

Two for One

The old 38 Dodge pickup gave me countless hours of enjoyment and I probably was able to put a couple hundred miles on it. I know that doesn't sound like much but I was only allowed to drive to the end of our dooryard and back which was about a tenth of a mile round trip. Granted, once in a while, I would get brave enough to sneak up to Dave's and drive through his fields but I always ended up losing track of time and getting caught. Dave never helped much either because he wanted to get his hands on that pickup and did all he could do to encourage me drive it to his place.

One day, when I was walking home from the poultry farm, I happened to notice that Dave had a couple of extra cars in his driveway and one looked like an honest to goodness doodle bug, something I was always going to make the old 38 into but never found the time. Besides that, driving was more fun than working, especially working on something that stood a good chance of never running. Moments later I was crawling all over the doodle bug and hitting

Dave with a hundred questions. Somehow Dave had traded something he no longer needed for these fine looking autos. One was a 53 Buick which was in really good shape but needed a starter and the other was a 53 Chevy which had been converted to a doodle bug. This old Chevy's body and frame had been cut right in half behind the front seat. The drive shaft had been shortened and the rear wheels were right behind the back of the front seat. To hold the roof up, a piece of plywood had been cut to fit with an oval hole in the middle of it to serve as a back window, minus the glass. Right above the rear wheels was a wooden box filled with concrete to add a little weight and sitting on the passenger floor was a five gallon gas can with a rubber hose running into it. In my eyes this 53 doddle bug was way cooler than Dave's and I knew I had to have it.

That was about the time Dave started in trying to trade the doodle bug for my old 38 and he almost had me but, I told him I first wanted to hear the engine run. Dave sat behind the steering wheel and turned the ignition switch and the old car fired to life and it sounded a lot like the fourth of July. It sat there bang, sputter, bang, bang, cough then quit. Dave said, "Yea, it could use a tune up but I know with your talent that would be a piece of cake." I didn't want to point out that he didn't know my talent all that well so I kinda agreed with him.

When dad drove into the dooryard that night, where the old 38 usually sat there was a doodle bug and out behind the barn, out of sight was a 53 Buick that didn't run. I met dad at the door and was so excited that I could hardly talk. I dragged him over to the 53 Chevy or I should say what was left of it and said, "What do you think of her?" He told me what he thought about her and I thought that was uncalled for, but decided not to say anything. I then fired the doodle bug up so he could hear it run and once again he told me what the thought about it. Then a smile came over his face. The only thing I can think is he must have figured the doodle would never get out of the dooryard on its own power.

For the next couple of weeks I worked on the old 53 every chance I got but it didn't seem to matter what I did to it. As soon as I started to drive it would go cough, bang, bang, cough and sometimes end with a big poof of smoke. In the meanwhile dad decided to have a culvert buried at the far end of the dooryard, in hopes that by diverting some of the water away from the ditch that followed the driveway, the dooryard wouldn't be so muddy in the spring.

On the first day that the culvert work began my cousin, Alan, showed up with a backhoe to dig the ditch in which the culvert would be laid. I was back working on my doodle bug and the moment Alan heard it run he came over and said, "It sounds like bad gas to me." So with that I took the five gallon gas can out of the front, filled dad's two lawn mowers, his rototiller and tractor. This almost emptied my gas can so I grabbed his fresh can of gas and filled mine.

Slowly but surely the doodle bug began to run better and better and soon all of the banging and coughing was gone and that old 53 was some fast. Again I met dad at the door when he got home that night and I wouldn't let him in the house until he tried my doodle bug. A smile came over his face when he heard how smooth it ran and slowly we drove out to the end of the driveway. Dad pushed the clutch in and we came to a stop, he shifted it into reverse and we started to back up. I said, "Step on it and see how much power this ole thing has." Dad stomped the gas pedal to the floor and we shot backwards like we had been shot from a sling shot. When we went by the barn dad stepped on the brake pedal only to discover that they went to the floor. "Oh yea", I said, "I got to work on the brakes next." That is when I remembered the ditch that Alan had dug that day. I looked out the back window and could see the pile of dirt, which was protecting the ditch, fast approaching. I looked at dad and he was wearing the same expression Dave had when we shot down the steep hill in Dave's doodle bug. Dad instantly slipped the car into neutral, double clutched it and crammed the shifting lever into first gear. He then put the gas pedal to the floor and popped the clutch. I soon saw the rear tires throwing dirt out the back as we continued to close the gap between us and the ditch. For a while all I could hear was a real loud screaming, that and the noise dad was making. We rode up to the top of the dirt pile before we came to a stop and slowly started to head back out of the driveway. Dad once again told me what he thought of my doodle bug.

Not much was said at the dinner table that night and after supper dad went out to mow the lawn. A few minutes later I stepped outside to start working on the brakes. As soon as I stepped out into the garage I could hear the lawn mower going bang, bang, cough, sputter and then quit. Dad was bent over trying to adjust the carburetor. I hollered out, "It sounds like bad gas to me."